Harvest of
Youth

Harvest of Youth

Jesse Stuart

Introduction by
Edwina Pendarvis

Jesse Stuart Foundation
1998

Harvest of Youth

Library of Congress Cataloging-in-Publication Data

Stuart, Jesse, 1907-
    Harvest of Youth / Jesse Stuart ; introduction by Edwina Pendarvis.
      p. cm.
    Contents: Out of the night -- Slabs from a sundown world -- Sonnets: juvenilia -- Harvest of youth.
    ISBN 0-945084-68-4
    1. Kentucky -- Poetry.   I. Title
PS3537.T92516H3   1998
811' .52--dc21

          98-12290
          CIP

Book Design by
JIM MARSH and BRETT NANCE

Published By:
The Jesse Stuart Foundation
P.O. Box 391 Ashland, KY 41114
(606) 329-5232 or 5233

Dedicated to
Harvey and Mae Dixon

Jesse, helping stack hay in rick.

Preface

In 1930, when twenty-four-year-old Jesse Stuart contracted with the Scroll Press in Howe, Oklahoma to publish a book of his poetry, *Harvest of Youth*, he could never have imagined his future successes as an author. This desperately poor, country boy from Greenup County, Kentucky would go on to publish more than sixty books, more than 460 short stories, and over 2000 poems in a writing career that began in 1930 and continues even today with the posthumous reissue of his out-of-print works and the publication of never-before-published manuscripts.

Nor could Stuart have envisioned the great and far-reaching success he would enjoy as a teacher. His impact was so enormous that highly-respected Stuart scholar J.R. LeMaster, Director of the American Studies Program at Baylor University, refers to Stuart as "the school teacher of America." Much of Kentucky's educational reform efforts of the last two decades was anticipated by Stuart, as shown in works like *The Thread That Runs So True*, *To Teach, To Love*, and *Mr. Gallion's School*.

For all of his writing successes, Stuart always saw himself as a teacher. "First, last, and always," wrote Stuart, "good teaching is forever, and the teacher is immortal." Certainly Stuart lives forever in the memories of tens of thousands of students whose lives he touched and inspired.

Two of those students were Kentucky natives Harvey and Mae Dixon, who married in Florida during World War II, while Harvey was serving in the Coast Guard, and then returned to Louisville after the war to begin careers as educators. In the fall of 1949, they moved to Bowling Green to continue their education at Western Kentucky University. Mae received her B.S. in 1950 and Harvey earned his bachelor's degree two years later, the same year that his wife earned her master's degree. During their stay at Western, the Dixons met Jesse Stuart through one of their English professors. Mae chose to write her M.A. thesis on Stuart.

From that point on, the Stuarts and the Dixons became life-long friends. Harvey and Mae had successful educational careers in Jefferson County, Kentucky, finally retiring in 1981 only to continue educational service for the next seventeen years as Consultants with World Book Educational Projects.

The Dixons and many other individuals made significant contributions to the beautiful book in your hands. Edwina Pendarvis, an Appalachian writer and professor at Marshall University in Huntington, West Virginia, copyedited the original text and crafted a fine Introduction. Brett Nance, a member of my office staff, designed the pages and made the book camera-ready. Jim Marsh designed the photo spreads and the dust jacket. However, no one contributed more than the Dixons, whose moral and financial support were essential to the success of this publication. Out of great respect for them and in deep appreciation for their support, the Jesse Stuart Foundation is proud to dedicate this book to our dear friends, Harvey and Mae Dixon.

James M. Gifford
Jesse Stuart Foundation
Executive Director

Contents

Introduction

Out of the Night

House on the Hill	37
What There Is to an Old House	38
Free God	40
Epitaphs:	
For Elmer Heaberlin	44
Poet	44
My Landlord	45
For J.Y.	45
And One not Dead	45
Know the Gypsy Wind Too Well	45
Last Lover	45
Consider the Poet	46
Mountain Funeral	46
Lilac Elegy	47
The Winner	48
Sleep	48
For Warriors Dead	49

Slabs from a Sundown World

River Railroad Man	53
Fantasy in Black	53
Undulated Seasons	54
Railroad Sounds	57
Silhouettes	58
Vagabond Houses	59
Black April	60
Initial-Scarred Trees	63
Steel Gang	65
My City	67

Sonnets: Juvenilia

Loneliness	75
My Loves Will Remain When I Have Passed	75
August Night	76
Batter Me Down, Life	76
To A Dissatisfied	77
To Edith	77
My Mountain Home	78
Clean Fingers Sloped in Farewell	78
To a Georgian Lass	79
Where I Was Born	79
Margaret	80
Returned	80
A Skeptic's Plea	81
Silent Earth	81
Heaven Enough	82
To Muddy Waters	82
It Will Not Matter Much	83
The Wind Has Ways	83
Louise	84
Old Lowland Meadows	84
Two Lives	85
Harvard or the Sea	85
To Calloye	86
Personae	86

Harvest of Youth

Harvest of Youth	91
Foreknown	91
Life's Inconstancy	92
Creed	92
To a Woman in Black	92
Youth	92
Saint or Sinner	93

Hurt Not the Proud	93
Words	93
My First True Love	94
Sin	95
Pity Me Not	96
One Life	96
Immodesty	96
Lincoln Weeps	97
Sleep Spell	97
My People's Prayers	97
Warnock Blues	98
Carver Life	99
Cool Fingers in Farewell	100
Empty Lover	101
Stanza on Leaving College	102
Disillusion	102
Weather	102
November Night	103
Tennessee Farmer	103
Aloha	104
My Brothers	105
My House	106
Finish	106
Scars	107
Spring Comes	107
She Ventured Far From God	107
Fugitive	108

Afterword

Honest Confession of a Literary Sin by Jesse Stuart

Dreamers' Solitudes

Blue Dreamers, you who lie beneath the dust,
Remember this: that while you lie beneath
The surface of the earth, the thin blue moon,
Not mindful now that pledged words are a trust,
Beams on you all alike in mother earth.
Remember, if you can: today at noon
We take the road you took through muck and mud
When you were builders of America;
We take the road to fight, to free our blood
From more oppressive chains than your dust knew.
And we shall see new brotherhood for man,
Or shed more blood before this thing is through.
Beam down, you moons, beam down upon our dead;
Blow over them, you winds, and words I've said.
Whine through the cornfields and the pasture woods
And find the dreamers in their solitudes.
Tell them that we are marching to the sun,
A new America before our march is done. *(SMP 98)*

Introduction

Beginnings

Like his ancestors, Jesse Stuart was a pioneer. With candor and simplicity, his writing helped to stake out new territory for poetry, which he saw as a land with plenty of room for everyone.

Stuart's democratic vision of poetry had everything to do with his eastern-Kentucky, working-class origins. He was born on August 8, 1906, in a one-room log house on a tenant farm near Riverton, Kentucky. In the wintertime, Jesse's father, Mitchell Stuart, worked in the small coal mines near Riverton, and in the summer he farmed. Year-round, his mother, Martha Hilton Stuart, did many of the outside chores and most of the housework: gardening, cleaning, cooking, sewing, even repairing the family's shoes. As he grew up, Stuart, too, worked hard on the farm. He planted, plowed, and harvested to help put food on the table. From the time he was ten or eleven years old, he added to the family's provisions by hunting squirrel, rabbit, and quail. In high school, he trapped minks and muskrats for their pelts, and he hewed crossties so he could buy his and his sister's schoolbooks.

In the midst of material hardship, Stuart learned at an early age the emotional hardship that a death in the family brings. In *Beyond Dark Hills*, his first autobiographical work, he tells about the death of one of his younger brothers:

> Herbert, the boy next to me, "took down" with pneumonia. I recall vividly the January day with a little bit of sun when my father sat on a box under a leafless apple tree. He wrung his hands, and said, 'It is too unbearable to stand. If we could have only had a doctor here in time to have saved him.' Another scene

I hate to recall was seeing a spring wagon with a pine box roped to the bed and two mules hitched to it…. We had to go five miles to my grandfather Hilton's farm for [the] burial…. We saw the fresh dirt thrown up near some pine trees. I remember the songs they sang, some of the words the preacher said. I remember how cold my feet got standing in the mud and how the people cried. *(BDH 46-47)*

In 1918, only a year or so after Herbert's death, Stuart's youngest brother, Martin, died of pneumonia, too. Before he was twelve years old, Stuart had lost two brothers, and he had become intimately acquainted with death.

Early confrontation with death is a formative experience in the lives of many artists and writers, who use their creative work to express their keen sense of death's immediacy. Their work is a way of immortalizing the people and things they love. But creating art requires emotional strength, and one source of Stuart's strength was his family's devotion to each other and to the land. The thought of death is frequently present in Jesse Stuart's poetry, but it is balanced by themes of endurance and passion for living. Eastern Kentucky farm life, after all, brought more than hard work. It brought freedom and pleasure. Stuart ran, climbed, and hid in the forested hillsides, and he swam in the creeks and rivers. Beauty filled his senses: He saw lilac trees in bloom and mist in the mountains; he heard autumn rains and wind in the tree tops; he smelled the clover-scented wind. Memories of these sensations fill his poems and stories.

Although the family was poor, the Stuarts shared simple pleasures. Good food was plentiful. His mother cooked and canned the corn, pumpkins, and beans they grew, and she made jams, jellies, and pies from their apples and peaches and from the blackberries that grew wild in the hollows. After supper, the family often sat and talked for hours—of owning their own farm someday, of the children's adventures at Plum Grove Elementary School, of local and national events. They told tales about their family and friends. These experiences, too, are relived in Stuart's poetry and prose.

From obscure rural beginnings, Stuart became one of the first southern Appalachian writers to earn worldwide literary acclaim. Although his reputation is based largely on his prose, he began his writing career as a poet, inspired by high school and college teachers and by the works of the great eighteenth-century Scottish poet, Robert Burns. We cannot fully understand Appalachian literature without coming to terms with the poetry of Jesse Stuart, and to come to terms with Stuart's poetry, the best place to start is at the beginning.

A Literary Sin

Harvest of Youth was Jesse Stuart's first book. That fact alone would make it significant even if it had nothing else to recommend it. Stuart was only twenty-four years old when *Harvest of Youth* was published in 1930 by Scroll Press in Howe, Oklahoma. By this time, he had already had several poems accepted by literary magazines. Two of the poems he used in *Harvest of Youth,* "Hurt Not the Proud" and "Sin," had already been published in a collection, *Braithwaite's Anthology,* along with poems by well-known authors Vachel Lindsay and Robert Frost. At the time he submitted this collection for publication, the author must have been proud of the poems, which he referred to many years later as his "high school, steel mill, and college poems written between the ages of fifteen and twenty-two" (SMP 3).

Soon after the book was published, however, Stuart himself destroyed most of the fifty copies sent to him by the publisher, for this first book was a terrible disappointment to him. Of the three hundred copies that Stuart had agreed to buy from Scroll Press, he bought only the first fifty. Because he burned many of his copies, less than two dozen remain, most in the hands of private collectors. Stuart describes his dismay at his first sight of this now-rare book:

> I knew that I had been swindled....I was really ashamed of my first book. It was published without a dust cover. There wasn't a single comment by a critic published in the book about what anyone had said about the merits of my first poems. I knew by reading well-published books, by name publishing houses...that my first published book was all wrong and I didn't want this. *(HY 113-114)*

Scroll Press was a vanity press, one of those presses to which authors can turn if they are willing to subsidize their own work by paying printing costs or agreeing to purchase all or most of the copies printed. This type of publication assists a writer eager to get in print a book that would have little chance of being accepted by a commercial press. When Stuart saw the shoddy workmanship of his published book and realized the full import of what he had done, he so regretted this venture he considered it a "literary sin."

Today, Stuart's sin does not seem so terrible. Like most young writers, he was eager to have his poems read, and his haste to publish his work is understandable. His later success as a writer has redeemed him. Moreover, in the last quarter of this century, the line between vanity presses and "legitimate" presses has blurred somewhat, due to a proliferation of small, regional publishers. To a large extent, these regional presses owe their existence to improvements in computer technology. Personal computers, laser printers, and computer-assisted design software have made high-quality book design and composition available to many more publishers than in the past. Jesse Stuart, who from the beginning desired to be a professional writer, felt that his having resorted to a vanity press was an undignified mistake. As an aspiring author, he wanted only "real" books by large—that is, New York and London—publishing houses. Now many small presses publish high-quality books. Now writers have more choices; they do not have to be published by one of a handful of major publishing corporations to have a "real" book. With the de-centralization of publishing, Stuart's "sin" no longer seems so great, though he was right in thinking his book substandard in appearance.

This volume of poems represents a significant event in Stuart's literary life, not just in being his first collection, but in having occasioned a "confession" from the author, whose literary "sin" was to have published his work through a vanity press. To shed further light on this incident in literary history, Stuart's essay about his experience, "An Honest Confession of a Literary Sin," has been included in this edition of *Harvest of Youth* as an afterword to the poems.

Harvest of Youth—the Collection

Stuart's position on *Harvest of Youth* must have softened later because he allowed the collection to be published by The Council of the Southern Mountains in 1964. In the introduction to the 1964 facsimile copy, Mace Crandall says:

> Some of the poems are marked more by youthful feeling than professional skills. Others reveal a maturity of concept and workmanship that was a signal of future proficiency…this book is a choice memento of days when 'Jesse Stuart' was not a name to be included in lists of American writers but merely the moniker for a husky high school and college lad who could love or fight or romp or grieve with abandon or sincerity equal to any occasion.

The early works of all major authors are important, and this first book of Jesse Stuart's is no exception. Many of his dominant themes emerge in these poems: His love of the land, his awareness of the presence of death in life, his respect for manual labor, and his sensitivity to human error. The poems in this collection *are* a wonderful memento of one of America's most famous writers, but they are of more than sentimental or historical interest. They're of literary interest, too. As Crandall says, many of them are surprisingly accomplished poems for so young and so relatively unschooled a poet as Stuart was at the time they were written. Perhaps the most striking feature of this collection is its haunted quality. This poignant quality is a signature of Jesse Stuart's poetry, and it is especially surprising to find in the work of so young a writer. Although there are touches of humor, a somber tone permeates the collection.

In his dedication to Harry Harrison Kroll, one of his English teachers at Lincoln Memorial University, the young Stuart refers to his first collection as "These Artless Poems," but he had reason to know that many of the poems were excellent. This reference to "artlessness" reappears in later poems, and it seems to express Stuart's commitment to truth and realism over considerations of style.

At the same time, *Harvest of Youth* is a consciously experimental work. In it Stuart attempts different poetic forms. Each of the four sections of the collection is different from the other, and each is interesting on its own terms as well as in relation to the book as a whole. In the first section, the quatrain—a four-line stanza historically associated with hymns and ballads—forms the basis for most of the poems. In the second, free verse predominates. In the third, sonnets are the primary form used. In the last section, the quatrain again takes precedence. The four sections of the book make a cyclic whole, and the four divisions foreshadow Stuart's frequent practice of dividing collections into the four seasons of the year. These poems represent many of Stuart's later stylistic techniques as well as the themes he continued to work throughout his career. If some of the poems are clearly the work of a novice, in every section there can be found many accomplished poems, including those which satisfied the author enough to be selected for later collections.

The dominant theme of this section is the search for identity. The writer's concerns are in making a home, finding a religion, developing character, and earning respect. All of the poems in this section, except the second poem, are about death, which provides the context for the search for identity.

Not surprisingly, among the quatrain forms used in this section is that form which is most directly related to death—the epitaph. The young Stuart must have been familiar with Robert Burns' satirical epitaphs, for example, this epitaph about a schoolteacher:

Here lie Willie Mickie's banes;
O Satan, when ye tak him,
Gie him the schulin' o' your weans,
For clever deils he'll mak them! *(Burns 196)*

This poetic form, traditionally used to comment on life and how it should (or shouldn't) be lived, indicates the importance of character and reputation for this eastern Kentucky youth. Stuart uses epitaphs to advise the living to enjoy life while they can and as a satiric means of criticizing people's folly. About a landlord, he writes:

He had the gold and three estates;
But when he had to pass
Life's finish line, he did not leave
His shadow on the grass. *(HY 45)*

In their concern with death, the poems in this section signify the human need to discover what things are most essential and to become dedicated to those things, to become an individual—to emerge out of the night.

The first poem of this section is one of the most interesting in its apparent ambivalence to values to which Stuart gives allegiance. The poem, "House on the Hill" tells about the devastating effects of misspent affection, but at the same time refuses to endorse conventional values completely. The poem is set at a widower's house where "Weeds choke the corn; the garden's dead;/ The burdock grows at the rotting sill"(37) The widower, who took good care of the house and grounds when his first wife was alive, has become an alcoholic because his second wife is unfaithful. Here, as throughout his poetic career, Stuart's work asserts the importance of family unity, of orderly homes, and well-tended land. (By the time this poem was published, *Home Circle* magazine had published his high-school essay on the value of well-kept yards.) Yet the author leaves the alcoholic widower unrepentant. His desire for the woman who has ruined him remains strong—"her white body haunts him still." (38)

While this poem points a moral about unwise love, it also acknowledges the power of the unattainable. The lonely longing in this poem is a strong force in Stuart's poetry. His poems often seem haunted by something unattainable, for which he cannot find adequate words, but which inspires his poetry. For Stuart, this feeling is closely associated with the restlessness of the wind. In *Beyond Dark Hills*, he says, "I can remember the way the wind howled around the shack and through the cedar tops. These scenes made me love loneliness…. It made one long for something beyond the hills" (40). He comments again in his account of his early life: "There was loneliness in the dark hills when wind stirred the withered leaves on the trees. It was music to me. It was poetry" (64).

"What There Is to an Old House" probably stems from a time when Stuart was teaching his younger sisters how to ride horseback. During one of their rides over the ridges, he saw the old log house at Cedar Riffles where he was born: "No one lived there now and a skunk denned under the floor. Birds built their nests under the eaves. Tall weeds grew beside the shack. The roof was leaking" (BDH 78).

In his poem about the homeplace, one of Stuart's most recurrent images—the wind—appears for the first time in this collection. In his work, as in the imaginations of many people, the wind is an elemental spirit—sometimes it brings good fortune and sometimes misfortune, but in this poem, as in Stuart's entire body of work, the wind is primarily a force for good. The old homeplace is desolate, and the narrator is the only human visitor:

> What there is to an old house,
>   I'm only left to know,
> Besides a hungry woodmouse
>   Besides a searching crow. *(38)*

But, near the end of the poem, "The singing winds begin to hum/ Above this old stone wall." The speaker is consoled by the wind and realizes that his memory of the house is important, so the refrain changes to

> And then, about this old house,
>   I know I'm left to know,
> More than a hungry woodmouse,
>   More than a searching crow. *(40)*

This consoling thought, the author implies, was born of the wind's song.

In many religions, including Christianity, supernatural power is represented by images of the wind. "Free God," a poem which presents the youth's questioning of orthodox religious doctrine and his seeking after God in nature says, "I found him in the winter wind," including the wind among other places in the natural world in which the young poet finds an animating spirit *(43)*.

The wind in Stuart's poems is often scented, as it is in "Mountain Funeral." This poem depicts the sorrow that rightfully accompanies the death of a steward of the land. The narrator, a guest who has come for the farmer's funeral, leaves the house where the corpse is lying and walks around the farm. Signs of the man's livelihood are all around: the blooming apple trees, the ax in the chop block, the plow, his bees "working on / His wind waves of clover" *(47)*. The presence of the things the man had cared about make his death more real. One of the most touching poems he ever wrote, "Mountain Funeral" had already appeared in *International Poetry Magazine* (October, 1929) when Stuart included it in *Harvest of Youth*. He also used this poem in his later collection, *Kentucky Is My Land* (1952), and the poem was reprinted by the *New York Sunday Times* in its October 19, 1952, review of *Kentucky Is My Land*.

"For Warriors Dead," perhaps the first of Stuart's many poems about Kentucky ancestors, is also about stewards of the land. If these ancestors returned, he says, they would find "not one cross bearing their long lost names" *(49)*. This poem concludes the section with a kind of epitaph for ancestors who had no tombstones. By describing them, Stuart brings them out of the night.

"Slabs From A Sundown World" (Section Two)

The title of the second section, "Slabs from a Sundown World," alludes to Carl Sandburg's 1922 poetry collection, *Slabs of the Sunburnt West*. "Slabs" must have meant several things to Stuart, but foremost in his mind were tombstones. He often visited the Plum Grove cemetery near his home. In his autobiography, he writes, "I must walk down among the moss-green slabs that mark the places of the sleeping Plum Grove dead" *(BDH 188)*. But the word "slabs" alludes to more than tombstones. The term is used in steel manufacture and in logging—industries which Stuart knew firsthand. In logging, a slab is the outside piece of the log left after the tree has been squared and sawn into boards. In steel-making, a slab is an iron or steel bar made by rolling an ingot so it is at least twice as wide as it is thick. This section of *Harvest of Youth* focuses on manual labor as well as on death resulting from the dangers of some types of labor. The concept of building, a concept that remained essential in Stuart's poetry as well as in his prose, is central to these poems. This section honors people who lost their lives struggling to build a better life for themselves and the people they loved.

"River Railroad Man" opens the section with a lament for a dead railroad worker. This poem shows the first use in the collection of what came to be one of Stuart's favorite poetic techniques—repetition of the first phrase of a line.

> His blood is in the smoke.
> His blood is in the steel.
> He heard mean winds strike the cold wirings on zero mornings,
> And whistle through the lonesome tree tops.
> He heard the moaning engines climb steep river grades
> And he heard the click of steel battering stell. (53)

In this poem, the repetition of phrases seems to mimic the rhythm of labor and of the trains themselves. Later in this and in other collections, he repeats words and phrases so consistently that this technique is a primary characteristic of all his poetry.

The second poem in this section, "Fantasy in Black," uses the builder theme and also harks back to the ruined-house as a metaphor for death and desolation. He writes

> And Rain and Death
> Swish through the doorway
> Of the hold I have built against the wind
> And the hosts of the air (53)

These lines suggest the ultimate futility of the builder's project. But the poem makes a positive assertion about the narrator with the words that follow: "I am an atom and a builder." Stuart acknowledges here that though his work may be doomed, he is a part of something larger than himself.

"Black April," the rural counterpart to these industrial poems, tells the story of Flint Sycamore, who builds his farm in W-Hollow. Battling crop failure and diseased horses, Flint finally succumbs to marshland fever. But, even as Flint fails, he also succeeds because his body becomes a source of beauty when the tall grass and a wild cherry tree grow out of the mound of his grave. The poem ends— "April life from the bosom of Flint Sycamore" *(63)*.

This second section contains the most imagistic poems in the collection. Though he later rejected imagism—a type of poetry which relies heavily on visual imagery and elliptical statement, the young poet handles this technique competently. "Silhouettes," is a mood piece, evoking the loneliness that seemed to haunt the young Stuart. "Vagabond Houses" conveys in sparse, imagistic style, Stuart's melancholy at the sight of abandoned or unkept houses.

"Steel Gang," a narrative poem about railroad workers, opens with one of the most compelling lines in Stuart's poetry:

Listen: we were dogging steel, somewhere, *(65)*

With its direct imperative to the audience to listen, and with its concentration on a single tragic event, this poem has ballad qualities without making use of the devices of rhyme and meter associated with ballads. This long, free-verse poem modernizes the ballad. In "Steel Gang," Stuart uses repetition and natural language to communicate the sense of tragedy familiar in old ballads. He tells the reader, "Now thirty men heard daily the whining engines," and "At night thirty men heard the strumming" *(66)*. Once more, he mentions the thirty laborers, "Thirty men worked all day in the smelt." At the end of the poem, after two men have been killed, and the men go back to their work, he emphasizes their absence through the changed refrain: "Now twenty-eight men hear daily the wheezing/ Engines, the rattling box-car doors…" *(67)*. Stuart's first-hand knowledge of the dangers of industrial labor and his respect for workers show clearly in this poem about working on the C&O Railroad.

Real, first-hand experience with the poetic subject was important to Stuart. In *Beyond Dark Hills*, the young writer reproaches Carl Sandburg for writing poems about steel laborers without knowing much about working with steel *(146)*. Stuart worked for ARMCO Steel in Ashland, Kentucky, after graduating from Greenup High School and before he went away to college in Tennessee. He speaks with unquestionable authority when he writes about grueling labor. "My City," the last poem in this section, also echoes Sandburg's work and may have been inspired by the older writer's poem, "Kalamazoo." In "My City," Stuart pays homage to his hometown of Riverton, Kentucky. "We came back to be a father's father's father,/ And a mother's mother's mother/ To blood unborn" *(70)*. In this poem, Stuart gives his readers more evidence of the value he placed on building a home and family.

"Sonnets: Juvenilia" (Section Three)

The sonnet was to become the form for which Stuart is best known. In these early sonnets, he meditates on his life and the choices he and his friends face. This section contains two poems that explicitly describe his youthful hopes and fears. "Two Lives" describes the tension between Jesse Stuart, the youth of action, and Jesse Stuart, the poet. As a member of the Greenup High School football squad, Stuart writes of the team:

> They fight, they drive, flinch not, for they are unafraid,
> And I belong to them, but moods in curious books
> Allure me far, with pen, to lonesome nooks. *(85)*

In this third section he also makes extensive use of the poetic technique of apostrophe, speaking directly to an absent person or object. This use of direct address allows him to give advice and, sometimes, to reproach his friends and neighbors.

In "Batter Me Down, Life," Stuart's imperative address is to life itself with all of its hardships. This poem has been compared to Carl Sandburg's "Prayers of Steel." But both Stuart's and Sandburg's poems may owe homage to John Donne's great sonnet, "Batter My

Heart." In this poem, Stuart welcomes struggle as necessary to living fully. His sonnet "To a Dissatisfied" offers emotional support to a rebellious friend or relative. Stuart wishes he could do more and says he would die if it would free the person. "I'd give my life for Life to set you free,/ And risk Proud Death's uncertain liberty." In his address to "My Mountain Home" he speaks to still another deserted house, one with lichened walls whose "haunting spirit" calls the narrator. "To Edith," "To a Georgian Lass," "Louise," and "To Calloye" are all written to girls the narrator has cared about. These poems regret the girls' absence and comment on their choices in life. With the exception of "To Edith," these sonnets come closest of all the sonnets to the kind of competent, but predictable, language that might be typical of any young man of his time.

One of Stuart's English instructors at Lincoln Memorial University told him she didn't like "To Muddy Waters." Her advice to him was to "Get away from sedge and muddy waters and the night wind" and to write "high, beautiful things like Shakespeare, Keats, Browning, and Longfellow" *(BDH 205)*. But Stuart couldn't have written so authentically about what the teacher regarded as high and beautiful things. More important, the things the teacher thought of as low and ugly were high and beautiful to this Appalachian writer. Stuart's love for the land is expressed more in these sonnets than in the other sections of this collection. In "Heaven Enough," he tells of his joy in eastern Kentucky's beauty:

Heaven for me will be an April field
With an orchard wind striding gallantly.
Heaven will be new Nature's rarest yield.
Each tree will be a gusty rain beat tree. *(82)*

In "Old Lowland Meadows," he acknowledges kinship with the animals in responding to the seasons: "Yes, there is charm when spring is in the boughs/ When kindred beast to kindred beast makes vows" *(84)*.

The sonnet form and the use of direct address lend themselves to his themes, and Stuart continued to use these devices to good effect in his second published collection of poetry, *Man With a Bull-Tongue Plow*. In this second published collection, he included five sonnets from this section of *Harvest of Youth*. "To Muddy Waters," "Batter Me Down, Life" and "My Love will Remain When I have Passed," are included as Sonnets 223-225. "My Mountain Home" became number 232, and "To Edith" with the title changed to "To B.G." became Sonnet 236.

"Harvest of Youth" (Section Four)

The last section of the book is the most uneven in quality. It has the most varied diction, including diction so archaic it strikes a discordant note. These poems reflect Stuart's admiration for other poets, particularly Robert Burns. Stuart first became acquainted with Burns in his sophomore year at Greenup High when his English teacher, Mrs. Robert Hatton, taught her favorite poet's work to Stuart's class. Stuart carried a copy of the "ploughman poet's" work everywhere, he says, and read it over and over again.

Robert Burns' life may have been of even greater importance to Stuart than Burns' poetry. Stuart says of Burns: "He was a Scottish plowboy. I read all about his life. I knew it didn't always take the boys that wore sweaters like Burl Mavis to do things. And my prayer if I ever prayed one then, was to write poetry that would endure like the poetry of Robert Burns" *(BDH 66)*. Stuart, a poor Scotch-Irish farm boy, must have been heartened by the success of this eighteenth-century farm boy from the mountains of Scotland. He saw from Burns' example that having fine clothes to wear and plenty of money to spend were not necessary for success in writing.

Stuart read Burns' poetry and wrote his first poems in the autumn of his sophomore year in high school. He read and wrote even while hunting opossums in the persimmon and pawpaw trees of

Greenup County. These earliest poems, some perhaps first written on the backs of poplar leaves, may be placed in this last section of *Harvest of Youth*. The poem, "Weather," which refers to the banks of the Clyde, a river in Scotland, almost surely comes from this period of Stuart's life. "Warnock Blues" with its "wee cot" and "rills" also bears the stamp of Robert Burns' diction. This poem may have been written while Stuart taught in a one-room high school in Warnock before going to Nashville, Tennessee, to Vanderbilt University Graduate School.

"My First True Love" is typical of the derivative poems in this section. It shows an irony similar to Thomas Hardy's poetic irony; its treatment of subject is similar to Burns' treatment; and its rhythms are reminiscent of some of Tennyson's poems. Stuart says that during the second summer of high school, he took a collection of Tennyson's poetry and a collection of Burns' poetry and went to live at Carter Caves, near Grayson, Kentucky. Of that summer, he writes, "I would sit at the mouth of a cool cave and read Tennyson for hours" *(BDH 71)*. Just as most artists learn by imitation, Stuart learned that way, too. His poetic diction, subjects, and rhythms show the influence of poets whose work he admired.

In this last section of the book, Stuart summarizes what life has taught him so far, what he has harvested. He makes use of the quatrain again, this time in summing up his personal views in several epigrams. The two poems from this section which were published in the *Braithwaite* anthology use this form. "Hurt Not the Proud" reminds the reader of the mortality of even the proud, who "Shall surely carve proud words in stone" *(93)*. "Sin" extols the virtues of sin as a means of learning about life and, ultimately, becoming wiser for it: "Better are young men who have sinned:/ They set their feet on firmer sod" *(95)* .

However, there is no single lesson here. Some of the aphorisms contradict others. Because of the various viewpoints put forth in these poems, this section calls to mind poet John Keats' concept of "negative capability," which manifests itself in all good writers. Negative capability is the capacity to live with doubt and uncertainty and to see things from more than one point of view. In this last section, Stuart shows this ability most strongly in his short poem "Lincoln Weeps" and in "My Brothers," his poem about soldiers buried at Flanders:

> I am wondering tonight, dear brothers,
> If you hear the patter of windless rain
> Beating cold Flanders sod and dying grass
> Where slowly you gave up the body's pain. *(105)*

"Blue Dreamer"

The epigraph which Stuart chose to use at the beginning of the First Edition of *Harvest of Youth* is prescient, in view of his later embarrassment over this publication:

> The poor inhabitant below
> Was quick to learn and wise to know
> And keenly felt the friendly glow
>   And softer flame;
> But thoughtless follies laid him low
>   And stained his name.

Son of an illiterate tenant farmer, Jesse Stuart *was* quick to learn. The first member of his family to graduate from college, he embraced literary life without rejecting his working-class roots. His father's illiteracy was no source of shame to him. He respected his father's way of life and his knowledge of farming and hunting. This prolific writer had nothing to apologize for, despite his regrets about his first publishing venture.

After this first collection, Stuart went on to become one of America's most revered chroniclers of Appalachian life. Called the most constant of the agrarian poets, he wrote loyally about things that were close to his rural home, and he wrote with conviction. He wrote about nature, but not as a disengaged observer. He had a sense of responsibility for nature and a sense of interaction with it. He wrote poetry from an environmentalist perspective and out of a skepticism about the value of what others call "progress" though it destroys the natural landscape.

With his poetic chronicles, Stuart tried to catch and hold life. He knew he couldn't, of course, and so the wind moves all through his poems. He uses it as a symbol for the inevitable passage of time. Given his early and constant awareness of death, Stuart showed great strength in his willingness to take on even a losing fight. In spite of his dismay at the thought of death, he was, to paraphrase one of his own phrases, a stubborn strainer at the heavy load *(AD 201)*. Sometimes discouraged by the lack of critical acclaim for his poetry, Stuart kept up the struggle to write poems to express his feelings. Because he was a straightforward, working-class man of passionate conviction from a culture with agrarian values, his poetry was destined to find little sympathy from urban publishers and critics committed to the modern poetic ideal of disengagement, cosmopolitanism, and subtlety. Today, more than a half-century since the publication of Stuart's first poems, his poetry retains its popularity with the public and is regaining the interest of critics, who are more willing to listen now to poetic voices expressing diverse political and personal views.

There is much to be discovered anew in his poems—his is such a compelling personality, and his work represents such a human struggle that questions of technique are of secondary importance. Stuart wrote with disarming honesty about large and small matters close to his heart. Sometimes generous-spirited and sometimes petty, he was always vital.

After a stroke which left him in a coma for two years, Stuart died in Ironton, Ohio, in February, 1984. But his hope that his poetry would endure seems certain to be fulfilled. After writing *Harvest of Youth*, he went on to write and publish many collections of poetry:

Man with A Bull-Tongue Plow (1934), *Album of Destiny* (1944), *Kentucky Is my Land* (1952), *Hold April* (1962), and *The World of Jesse Stuart: Selected Poems* (1975). Another compilation, *Songs of a Mountain Plowman* (1986), was published after his death. He will be to other young writers what Robert Burns was to him, a plowman singing at the plow. Fashions in poetry come and go, but many people will continue to cherish Stuart's work because it is about the essentials of their lives.

This collection of early poems shows the literary promise of a boy who spent his childhood roaming the hills of eastern Kentucky, listening to foxes and screech owls, to the river and the wind. His translation of the sounds and images of his youth is now a crucial element in Appalachia's literary heritage. No one interested in the history of Appalachian literature can ignore him, and no one who is knowledgeable about Appalachian culture can doubt the authenticity and authority of his voice. Stuart has become one of the "blue dreamers" of the literary world. His first collection, *Harvest of Youth*, captures a small part of a certain place and a time that will never come again.

Edwina Pendarvis
Huntington, West Virginia

Works Cited

Burns, Robert. *The Complete Poetical Works of Robert Burns*. Eds. W.E. Henley and T.F. Henderson. Cambridge, MA: 1897.

Stuart, Jesse. *Album of Destiny*. Mt. Vernon, NY: S.A. Jacobs, The Golden Eagle Press, 1944.

___. *Beyond Dark Hills*. 1938. Ashland, KY: The Jesse Stuart Foundation, 1996.

___. *Harvest of Youth*. 1930. Berea, KY: Council of the Southern Mountains, 1964.

___. *Kentucky is my Land*. 1952. Ashland, KY: The Jesse Stuart Foundation, 1992.

___. *Man with a Bull-Tongue Plow*. 1934. New York: E.P. Dutton & Co, 1959.

___. *Songs of a Mountain Plowman*. Ashland, KY: Jesse Stuart Foundation, 1986.

___. *The World of Jesse Stuart: Selected Poems*. Ed. J.R. LeMaster. New York: McGraw-Hill, 1975.

Burns, Robert. *The Complete Poetical Works of Robert Burns.* Eds. W.E. Henley and T.F. Henderson. Cambridge, MA: 1897.

Clarke, Mary Washington. *Jesse Stuart's Kentucky.* NY: McGraw-Hill, 1968

LeMaster, J.R. *Jesse Stuart: Kentucky's Chronicler-Poet.* Memphis, TN: Memphis State U P, 1980.

LeMaster, J.R. "Jesse Stuart's Poetry as Fugitive-Agrarian Synthesis." In J.R. LeMaster and Mary Washington Clarke, eds., *Jesse Stuart: Essays on His Work.* Lexington: U of Kentucky P, 1977: 19-39.

Stuart, Jesse. *Album of Destiny.* Mt. Vernon, NY: S.A. Jacobs, The Golden Eagle Press, 1944.

___. *Beyond Dark Hills.* 1938. Ashland, KY: The Jesse Stuart Foundation, 1996.

___. *Harvest of Youth.* 1930. Berea, KY: Council of the Southern Mountains, 1964.

___. *Kentucky is my Land.* 1952. Ashland, KY: The Jesse Stuart Foundation, 1992.

___. *Man with a Bull-Tongue Plow.* 1934. New York: E.P. Dutton & Co, 1959.

___. *Songs of a Mountain Plowman.* Ashland, KY: Jesse Stuart Foundation, 1986.

___. *The World of Jesse Stuart: Selected Poems.* Ed. J.R. LeMaster. New York: McGraw-Hill, 1975.

(From Jesse: The Biography of an American Writer, by H. Edward Richardson, McGraw-Hill, 1984)

Plum Grove School, 1917. Jesse is on the extreme right of the bottom row. His sister Sophia is standing center back row. Miss Elta Copper, teacher.

From left, Jesse with senior classmates Oscar Sammons, Thurman Darby and James D. McCoy.

(Courtesy The Jesse Stuart Foundation)

*se with sister Glennis—the oldest and youngest of
:hell and Martha Stuart's children—ca. 1926.*

Out of the Night

Greenup High School sophomore class, 1923-24.
Stuart front row, far right.

Greenup High School senior class, 1925-26.
Stuart back row, far left.

HOUSE ON THE HILL

What's become of the house on the hill?
Weeds choke the corn; the garden's dead;
The burdock grows at the rotting sill;
Smart weeds grow in the tulip bed
Life too has grown curiously still
Since something is wrong on the hill.

Last spring we knew how Lucy kept
The yards alive, the hedge in trim,
The garden clean, the walkways swept,
And how she did the chores for him
Who worked till nine before he slept:
The way man passes time unwept.

Now John is dead since Lucy died.
Once things went well and he went right,
But then he wed the other bride
Who snarls him with her subtle might.
He never says a gay good-night,
He pauses time in moody light.

She grew so wily she would dare
To go to town and go alone
With Lucy's tulips in her hair.
Since she had now some bolder grown
John sat at home and sat alone
Obeying her defiant tone.

She thought that Lucy's ways were vain.
What Lucy did she would not do.
She found his faults with much disdain;

He lost heart trying, lost her too:
His fate was near. He fell into
Strange company and careless grew.

While now he drinks to drown his care;
One life he thinks–I live today–
He dreams of her in the old house there
A girl so different to his way.
Strange to think people would say:
"He'll be alright with her away."

Here's what's wrong with the house on the hill:
Why the corn's unkept and the garden dead;
Why burdock grows at the rotting sill;
Why smart weeds grow in the tulip bed;
The saloon is his desire for ill
Since her white body haunts him still.

WHAT THERE IS TO AN OLD HOUSE

What there is to an old house,
    I'm only left to know;
Besides a hungry woodmouse,
    Besides a searching crow.

It is merely lichened walls
    Of an unsheathed ruin,
With two or five division stalls
    And the roof dropping in.

And it is but the trash place
    In a remote abode
Where wanderers of a lost race
    Throw down a heavy load.

Now I can see the old stove
    With legs rusted red;
I can hear the oven shove
    And the children beg bread.

I can see the old hearth
    With the heat wide flung,
With the fire's crackling mirth
    Where the pot hooks swung.

There's something to an old house
    I'm only left to know,
Besides a hungry woodmouse,
    Besides a searching crow.

For here is mother's ketch-all
    Swinging full of rags,
With her moth eaten shawl
    And some old rug bags.

For here's a bent apple tree
    With our old rope swing;
With the leaves tossing free
    Where the orioles sing.

For here is a swinging door
    That once was barred
With this prop on the floor
    When the winds blew hard.

And now sickly autumn comes
    And the shadows fall:
The singing winds begin to hum
    Above this old stone wall.

I have heard the deep, deep song
    Of the long, long ago;
The deep song and long, long,
    Of unforgotten woe.

And then, about this old house,
    I know I'm left to know,
More than a hungry woodmouse,
    More than a searching crow.

FREE GOD

While I was yet a young child
    I heard an old man pray
For his Saviour to come down
    And bear our souls away.

To bear our white souls away,
    To bury sinful flesh,
From the white winged angels
    And elemented mesh.

He told us his Saviour wore
    A halo round his head;
He told us that Judas' beard
    Was of deceitful red;

And when we got to Heaven,
   How we would understand
How the Saviour went walking
   With a cane in his hand.

Then the eyes of the people
   Were lit with fiery glow,
When he pointed his finger
   Each brother nodded, "So."

I believed I heard God's word;
   I formed my belief
From the prelude of wind words
   From the crisp dry leaf.

I surrendered to the God
   That the old man knew;
I dared risk my own thought
   And read the Bible through.

For I was yet a young lad,
   And I spake as a child,
Attentive as an old man
   After he has run wild.

Then I met with Youthful Sin
   And he threw wide his door;
He bade me walk freely in
   And love him to the core.

I loved a free, fast life,
   I loved Youthful Sin;
And when his door was open,
   Freely I walked in.

What if I were wild and free;
    For scarcely any man
Can become the quietless quiet
    The strictly Puritan;

What if I were wild and free;
    There was no God to care,
For rebellion in my flesh,
    And heart's rebellious lair.

I didn't care if God's commands
    Were twenty and seven;
I didn't care for angel shouts
    All over God's Heaven.

Youthful Sin had come my way:
    He told me to begin;
He threw wide his lattice doors
    And I went freely in.

And then the old women said:
    "Poor child's gone astray,
But he'll come to God again
    If we will only pray."

Why should I care if Jesus
    Wore haloes round his head?
Why should I care if Judas' beard
    Were of deceitful red?

For the God that I had known
    I was a fool to love.
When each day brought no return
    From his stale love thereof.

I lived with Youthful Sin
    With life stained yellow;
So one stark terror night
    I left my bed fellow…

With Sin I'd slept a long night
    In an ominous rain,
Thinking of a free, fast life
    And with God on my brain.

I forgot the word prelude;
    I forgot the dry leaf;
I forgot the idle God:
    I formed my belief.

I read my dusty Bible
    From cover to cover;
I found one God and one God
    Was a jealous Lover.

He was a Jealous Lover:
    And I a fool for Love;
When I read into His word
    My heart grew full thereof.

And the one God and one God
    Was with me all the time;
He was a mild God, a free God;
    He was apple tree slime.

I found him in the rising sap
    In a March sapling tree;
I found him in the winter wind,
    Blowing wildly and free.

I found him in the water;
   I found him in the air;
I found him in Sinful flesh;
   I found him everywhere

He had a tremendous soul
   Of all under the sun.
And the bloods of his people
   Were to Him as one.

And I make my vows for his love
   And from sin to recover
And to calm rebellious flesh
   Of any sinful lover.

Epitaphs

FOR ELMER HEABERLIN

If Heaberlin's Loves come to him here,
   Forget the words: "I love you so."
Flesh bearing rank, scholastic grain
   Within some weeds will surely grow.

POET

If there is life beyond the grave,
   He lives in future bliss.
If there is not another world,
   He made the most of this.

MY LANDLORD

He had the gold and three estates;
But when he had to pass
Life's finish line, he did not leave
His shadow on the grass.

FOR J.Y.

They hauled her here from West Birmingham
    But the neighbors did not know
When they earthed her down upon her grave
    A tree with tongues would grow.

AND ONE NOT DEAD

He has such rare and radiant face
    The angels down in Hell,
Who fell from that all perfect place,
    Will wonder why he fell.

I KNOW THE GYPSY WIND TOO WELL

I know the gypsy wind too well.
    On her a dream I made.
While yesterday she blew me sun,
    Today she blows me shade.

LAST LOVER

I know that Earth will be my last lover.
    To kiss her lips will not disturb my will;
For others lie with her under cover,
    Lie with her curiously still.

CONSIDER THE POET

(FOR ROLAND CARTER)

Go back to earth and note how well
    Sweet grass will grow beneath your feet.
Touch it to see if grass will tell
    Temper in a different heat.

Go where the sympathetic rain
    Forgets to quench an underfire,
Rain drenched in and out again
    Lost in the wonderment of desire.

Go back to earth where many years
    Have dimmed his lettered stone;
Bend low to give a poet poet's tears
    For earth will claim you for her own.

MOUNTAIN FUNERAL

We could not stay about the house
    Where so many were crying.
We pushed away from the sobbing crowd,
    From where the corpse was lying.

We walked down the back yard pathway
    Among his blooming apple trees,
And wondered about his season's dreams
    Of gathering fruit from these.

His lank bay mules he used in plowing
    The sandy upland loam
Played in the willow shaded barnlot
    Before his mountain home.

His rusty ax stuck in the chop block,
    In the furrow set his plow:
And warm wrought hands that used them
    Lie cold and lifeless now.

And the bees he loved were working on
    His wind waves of clover.
The evening winds he loved to hear
    Were softly blowing over.

But soon, too soon, soft voices were singing:
    "Dan Webber's days are o'er.
And now he sleeps…forever sleeps…
    And walks and talks no more."

We remembered his blooming apple trees
    His ax, his plow, his clover–
And the evening winds he loved to hear
    Softly blowing over.

LILAC ELEGY

She had to learn how hard it is to wait
The afterwhiles time made her dribble fate.
She was an exile no tears could appease,
Cautiously she gathered lilac trees,
Transplanted them in earthbound rows
Where the Gypsy Wind blows.

O exiled Mother of Earth! O she is dead!
The lilac winds are choking in my head.
And times I may repass this way again
Music will be recurrent on my brain…
Malignant hands in the lilac bough
Never so cold as now.

THE WINNER

Against his will he ran a race with Death.
    His muscles were taut drawn in every limb.
His team mates saw him falter…lose his breath…
    They sought to cheer when Death romped by him.

SLEEP

There are seconds in our lives that pass
Us down long, dark alley ways of dreams.
We drift like leaves on currentless streams
Out beyond all time and whirling mass
Of space. And softly we sink, and deep
Beyond all time and where all time is vain,
Where we give up the body and the brain
And lie in peace in our dead sleep.

Then what is sleep when seconds take
Us without the body's will or strong embrace
Of mind? And whether our sleep shall break
Or last, there is no one here to tell…
We only know we sleep and then farewell.

FOR WARRIORS DEAD

If warriors' bones should rise from forlorn hills,
Assume colourful flesh and brittle blood,
Forget the death dance, the fife's whirring shrills,
Forget thin, cool wrappers of writhing mud,
They would find cloistered houses rich in change,
Treeless hills bent in tawny sun-down flames;
They would find new kin, defiant, proud, yet strange–
But not one cross bearing their long-lost names.

The Grant-Lee Sr. Literary Society

OFFICERS

ROY MANLEY - - - - - - - - - - - - - - - *President*
JESSE STUART - - - - - - - - - *Vice-President*
LUTHER CARSON - - - - - - - *Secretary*

ROLL

CHARLES SNAVELY
MAURY MITCHELL
JESSE STUART
MASON GARDNER
ROBERT CARTER
DONALD WEST
PAUL DYKES
ROLAND CARTER
D. V. REDMOND
OTTO RHEBERG
RUE DALTON
ERNEST FIELDS

JOE B. JOHNSON
LUTHER CARSON
DUDLEY HUMAN
BRUCE HENDRON
HOWARD WADELL
CONLEY DICKERSON
ROY MANLEY
MORRIS HAIR
"DOC" HAIR
W. A. BIGGART
W. M. MILHOUSE
JENKINS

*Jesse Stuart and friend
Don West at LMU.*

Slabs from a Sundown World

Jesse and his dog Frisk, 1937.

Jesse Stuart salting his sheep, 1938.

River railroad man

Shovel under this old river railroad man with reverence.
He slept river nights of his life working
After days of work on river railroads.
Now he goes to his long sleep.
Still, heavy trains sweep on to their destiny
For his life is in them and lives.
His blood is in the smoke.
His blood is in the steel.
He heard mean winds strike the cold wiring on zero mornings,
And whistle through the lonesome tree tops.
He heard moaning engines climb steep river grades
And he heard the click of steel battering steel.
Now these same sounds that once he heard
Will continue to whine over his cool tomb
Where he will lie cold
And dream of picks and shovels.

Fantasy in black

When Tomorrow has come
And Rain and Death
Swish through the doorway
Of the hold I have built against the wind
And the hosts of the air,
There will be but emptiness and night
Since I am an atom and a builder.
I have lived at the muddy root of life
Deep set under the rock of time.
And I did not know that now
Is the time of all times;
That today is yesterday,
The inch of our future.

UNDULATED SEASON

I

i met her a tiny flame
in a tiny town that hath not understanding
when March tree sap
was turbulent young blood
in young arteries
when prophetic March winds sang
through the white plum leaves
drank the sweets from her body
the world is young
    and you are young and free
    as sap in March wood veins
    drink the sweet from her body
    feast while you may

2

copper August
myriads of grass
with tawny arms clutching
dry concrete breasts for nourishment
papers and the wind hither and thither
down monuments
dark alley ways
called time

3

a tiny flame in a tiny town
lies limb to limb with any lover
    the world is young
    and you are young
    feast while you may

4

nasal Autumn
tweaking winds in bare twigs
plum leaves in a golden shower
rustle with the wind
down alleyways
called time
    birds fly to bare plum twigs
    to chat of love
    one by one they come
    remembering the glossy green
    of their season
    mating

5

now the old men talk
where is she now
gone is she
who was so beautiful

we knew her
but she is gone
we dare not speak of her
we dare not speak for her
since she is gone

6

yellow the winds drift
the winds drift yellow
time is strewn yellow with plum leaves
footprints of school children

innocent metallic imprints
are buried under
for the old to see
a town hath not understanding

7

winter of life
an undulated season
for storms age sap
but winter has drunk
the sap from summer's warm sweet body
    there was a season
    when the world was young
    God planned it
    not i

8

my little flame in a little town
a cool thin smoke
streams up from her body
storms turbulent
wreck her grave
currents leapt to scar it
muddy water currents
the yellow winds blow over
and over
then snow piles high
the world is clean
so the old men say who remember
sins of the world buried
snow piled
clean

9

a tiny flame in a tiny town
lies limb to limb with any lover

10

and
if sterility
a lover Death
will question
surely

RAILROAD SOUNDS

I have heard mean groans of heavy engines
Striking the emptiness of night.
And I have heard the drive wheels slipping
At Black Mountain when the track was sanded.
Those sounds I have heard and loved.

I have heard the lonesome whistle screaming
When a bright was leading,
A red light trailing,
And the naked train moaned with the wind.

I have heard the oozing steam from slick pistons,
The swinging, and banging of box car doors;
And I have heard the winter winds
Whip the frozen wiring
And tear across the bitter sky.
These sounds I have loved.

But when
    the depot crowd begins to gather
And the train moves on,
I hate to hear friends and lovers say:
"Good-bye till we meet again…Good-bye."

SILHOUETTES

Hard, clean,
Chiseled profiles
Of black bodied trees
Swerving in the wind
At sundown.

Cold etchings…
Winter surface washed hills
Rim-cutting a chalk gray
Skyline…

And last a leaning
Lean-to shack
Pressing the dark…

Only these
Silhouettes...

VAGABOND HOUSES

This town is old
And sleepy
With red lights
Cutting
Against the dark.

The houses
Are cripples;
Aged vagabonds
Resting by a road
Leading somewhere.

Slow sinking roofs
Are thatched…
Loose doors
Flung to the wind
Bang emphatically.

Gaunt…
Huge…
Mystic…
City of souls,
Black drops of ink
Resting by a road
Leading somewhere.

BLACK APRIL

Only God
Could beat Flint Sycamore
When he played his last trump:
In the loam he battled for bread.

In March
Flint moved to W-Hollow
In a two horse surrey,
His wife, Lucy, by his side.

He drove
A white horse with black feet,
A black horse with white feet,
Until sundown
On a third day.

Flint stopped the horses,
Tied two loose leather reins
To two white pine tree roots;
He sifted pine tree loam
Through his scrawny fingers…
"A place to build," he said.

He fed the horses corn
From the two horse surrey,
Tied them a rope's length to graze.
Lucy broiled a ham supper
From a pine cone fire.

They bedded in the open,
In the freedom of space…
Only the wind in the pine tops,

The horses' neighs
The lone wolf's howl,
And the caw caws of dreaming crows
In the black tree tops:
These, for resonant tones…

Morning.
Flint pitched a pine pole house,
A wind structure
Daring a pavilion of wind.

He unbeveled his ax
From an emory piece,
Felled trees for corn space.
Lucy daubed the pine pole house
With mud and sticks
Against the wind and tomorrow.

Flint Sycamore planted April corn:
In the loam he battled for bread.
Spring was late; April, black…
Corn rotted in the ground;
Potatoes lay under dogwood surf;
Cane never sprouted at all…

The crows sang caw caws to the wind
And to each other…
They built nests of pine pole limbs
And daubed the cracks with mud and sticks.
The crows laughed
And the winds sang…

Flint Sycamore said:
"God, I'll beat you yet."
His first born came
A mangled mass
Of malgamated
Blood and dust…

The crows laughed and sang
To the wind and to each other;
For they too had built a house.
The horses ate
An incredible variety of plants,
Took the murrain,
Were left a stench upon the wind.

Black April…

Flint staggered back:
"God I'll beat you yet."
God beat Flint Sycamore.
His marshland fever
Cut Flint down
Like a weed in autumn.

Down in a meadow
Where two dim lettered
Lichen sandstones
Are marveled at by
Long gray lines of
Traffic comers, goers;
Sleeps Flint Sycamore.

• • •

Twelve men,
Are sitting at a picnic table
White clothed
With rarest food.
Life is a pleasure they say,
And God is kind.

They look at the green meadow
And the dim lettered lichen stones
Shaded by a tall grass of undying beauty:
Shaded with a wild cherry
With a thousand white sprays

Daring the wind…
Life from the richest earth;
Life from a daring dust;
April life from the bosom
Of Flint Sycamore.

INITIAL-SCARRED TREES

I.

These aged trees are dear to some one.
These giant clustered trees,
Lonely intitial-scarred
With chiseled forms of iron tracery
Swaying high in the high winds.

II.

Long, long years ago lovers came here
Wandering down this rocky lane
Where the road and the brook
Fought for a right of way,
And the sun
Left drying pools of standing water
Dotted with first fallen sun-cupped leaves.
Lovers came where the blue star-grass
Waved anod in the wind,
Waved in zigzag corners of an old rail fence;
And lovers came where the high winds surged
Through the lonesome giant clustered tree tops,
Like the lapping January waters
Along a frozen river shore.

III.

They stopped and cut their initials here,
Maybe for a fond remembrance,
Maybe to tell a secret, to tell of love.
But better yet for nothing at all.
Perhaps there is something
They will remember some day
When they return with their children
And their children's children.
They will remember the blue-star grass
Anod in the wind by the old rail fence;
They may remember the dried up brook
With standing pools of shadowy water
And the first fallen sun-cupped leaves;
And they may remember the high winds'
Deep surge through the lonesome tree tops.

IV.

But the years come
And record their names and numbers.
So many are born and so many pass away…
Population drifts; population fades away…
And only the new comers ask:
"What about the past,
The dreams and ashes of the past–
What of it anyway?"
Only these hieroglyphics remain;
These initial-scarred trees
Swaying high in a pavilion of wind…
Trees telling a history, telling a past,
Of ten years, fifty years, of a century,
When the initial bearers have long been dust.

STEEL GANG

Listen: we were dogging steel, somewhere,
Between Six Hickories and Muldraugh Hill…
Daring, stormy…we chewed tobacco and flapped
Broad-rimmed and dusky felt hats…
Six Hickories, a town of seven families
Crouched in the shadow of Big Horn Mountain…
Empty and gaunt…

The C and O Railroad twists slowly over
The flanks of Big Horn Mountain…the C and O
Railroad…dun and gray the color of
A copperhead turned on his back to die…
We got mail twice a day delivered by
The east and the west bound passenger trains.

We could hear the rattling box cars,
The wheezing engine straining every nerve
And a shower of fine pebbles droning against
The black earth as the long freighter rolled
Over the flanks of Big Horn Mountain.

Now thirty men heard daily the wheezing engines,
The rattling of the box car doors, the droning
Pebbles and the whistles, long and lonesome,
When the freighters rolled over the flanks
Of Big Horn Mountain.

At night thirty men heard the strumming
Of a Jew's harp and the songs of long ago.
They sang "John Henry," I'll Be All Smiles Tonight"
And "Shout All Over God's Heaven."

Thirty men worked all day in the smelt of
A drizzling rain–of a rain that made
The railroad tools cold and gummy.

But listen: the doggs slipped; the rail fell.
Five men under…five men arose but two fell
Again…Howland and Smith…wiped blood from
Their hair…cursed God and died…
Five men carried away the dead men wrapped
In cold and gummy sacks…

We dug a grave on Big Horn Mountain…we dug
It with sticks…Threw ashes in the dead men's
Faces and buried them with our picks and shovels.
We said a prayer…sang "Shout All Over God's Heaven,"
And five men returned.

Now twenty eight men hear daily the wheezing
Engines, the rattling box car doors–a shower
Of fine pebbles drone against the black earth when
The long freighters roll over the flanks of
Big Horn Mountain…they hear the strumming of
A Jew's harp and the songs of the long ago.

MY CITY

Riverton, my city, of two hundred houses
Was built when the Ohio Valley was young,
In the dawn change of clean sky mists
By new men of a new West
Who had a dream to build a city.
First, the town was a germ,
And then a plant that grew and grew.
The new born came and the river blood was in them.
The old passed away and were buried
In the hovering shadows of changing clean sky mists
Where the soft winds hummed old plantation songs,
Low and lonesome, like red moons on river nights,
Songs for the long sleepers…

Riverton, my city, had her dirty wharf boat landing
Where Saturday loafers ganged for the east bound passenger boat;
The Grey Hound wending from St. Louis on the west
To Pittsburgh in the east…
Men that had nothing to do,
Waited for the lonesome whistle
When the winds sang through the river cornfields
Old plantation songs without words…
Riverton had her one room post office

Where two cobble stone streets met.
Octagon sided, wind leant,
Under twelve honey locust trees.

Here mail came twice a week
    Once from the east,
    Once from the west,
And was delivered in a two-horse surrey…

And the old men loved my city…
The old men who passed away
And were buried in the shadows
Of Ohio river mists…
The new born loved my city
For the river blood was in them.
They grew up here and went to see the world
But they returned to where the red moon
Rose in velvet clouds
And hung above the low black hills
In late evening,
And above the court house square at midnight.
How could the sleepers forget these moons
When the soft winds sang through the river cornfields
Old plantation songs of the long ago?
Here my generation was born
And we know my city and her people.

My father's father's father told my father
And he gave me the secret,
And I know my people…
They knew the sleepers in the shadow
Of the changing clean sky mists…
They knew the singers and the songs they sang…

Voice of the old, silent now, and the corn
Waves from their bosom…
My father's father's father
And his father's father are there
Buried where the winds sing soft and lonesome…

We loafed at the dirty wharf boat landing
And the pine pole school house,
And played tag on the cobble stone streets
By the octagon sided post office
We loafed where the red moon circles the velvet sky
At midnight above a city of two hundred houses,
Above the court house square…
Elmer, Bert, Estille, James, Oscar, Thurman;
Edith, Grace, Irene, Jaunita, Elizabeth, Kyon…
We loved our youth, our city…
But we wanted to go somewhere,
To Pittsburgh, to St. Louis.
We grew tired of our city.
We wanted life
What were red moons and river nights
And the old plantation tunes,
And a place the dead remembered?

We went to the dirty wharf boat landing
So tired of being tired
And bought tickets for Pittsburgh in the east
St. Louis in the west…
Elmer, Bert, James, Oscar, Thurman;
Edith, Grace, Irene, Jaunita, Elizabeth, Kyon…
Proud, bent, daring, to go,
From a town of two hundred houses
To see the world.

We left with a long good-bye
To make a dream and build a city.
We went to meet life.

We saw Pittsburgh and St. Louis
And they were like Riverton
Only the winds there didn't remember the sleeping dead
And the red moons were not the same,
Nor were the post office and the court house square…
So we grew tired of St. Louis and Pittsburgh
And proud of Riverton
Proud to be loafers
At the dirty wharf boat landing,
Proud to play in our cobble stone streets,
Proud of our blood and our sleeping dead.
So we came back one by one:
We had seen Pittsburgh and St. Louis;
And they were like Riverton.
We came back to be
A father's father's father,
And a mother's mother's mother
To blood unborn.
We loved the city where the wind loved the dead,
For there was no other city like it.
We loved our blood for there was no other like it;
In a city the dead remember,
In a city where the wind loves the dead.

"Sir, I am a farmer singing at the plow..." Jesse Stuart

JESSE HILTON STUART
RIVERTON, KY.
BACHELOR OF ARTS

Gamma Lambda Sigma '26-'27-'28-'29, Vice-President '26, Secretary '27, Treasurer '28, Art Critic '29; Glee Club '27; Track '28-'29; Kentucky Club '27-'28-'29, Vice-President '28; Student Volunteer Band '27-'28, Treasurer '27, Secretary '28; Y.M.C.A. '27-'28; Dramatic Club '29; Writer's Club '29; Blue and Gray '26-'27-'28-'29, Editor-in-Chief '28-'29.

He does not need the spectacles of books to read nature. He does not need the precedent of others intellect to be intellectual. He conquers adversity with the same zeal that he enjoys prosperity. In this aspiring, determined man genius does not lie dormant. In the future Stuart must inevitably occupy the Pinnacle with America's greatest poets.

"What price Glory?"

Sonnets: Juvenilia

A frustrated young Jesse

"I wanted something I could no longer find in the hills....flashy colors, parties, romance...."

(Courtesy H. Edward Richardson Collection, Ekstrom Library, University of Louisville)

LONELINESS

I still remember when you went away
On that red morning in the summer drouth,
When dry winds blew from out the lonely south;
I still remember all you had to say.
Vines then that draped the cottage wall
Have turned buff colored in the sun;
Beech leaves are slowly dropping one by one;
And south-going birds only stop to call.
The loneliness and Life's little things bring back
You to me again. The ghosts of autumn rains
Tapping the roof, beating the window panes,
Gambling with Night's deserted waste of black,
I cannot forget. My life is lost in you
As azure skies are lost in windless blue.

MY LOVES WILL
REMAIN WHEN I HAVE PASSED

My loves will remain when I have passed
Beyond this certainty of time and light
And positive decay. But surely this night
I shall remember. These spiral massed
Pine silhouettes against the horizon.
Nocturnal things have been my loves: moon-downs,
Valleys of fog and sleepy mountain towns,
Dew on the grass and play of wind upon
The hill. Night sounds I have loved: the cold
Nosing winds in November corn stubbles;
The zoom of wires and water that troubles
Creek mosses and ferns. Happier loves will unfold
When I have passed far beyond this night.
Beyond all loves and swimming time of light.

AUGUST NIGHT

No night shall come like this again
When rent clouds are ledged and thinned,
And the quiet stirs of August wind
Blow through the trees cool wisps of rain.
There ghosts of rain are far more kind
Than winds of a soft midsummer noon.
But there shall come and shall come soon
Time when one shall be left behind.
You say, you know, it is not soon
As we watch thin clouds of rising fog
Drawn from low valleys by the moon.
But we listen to a shrill voiced frog,
Knowing one night is left behind
And youth is gone that once was kind.

BATTER ME DOWN, LIFE

Batter me down, you who are strong, I plead.
I, who am weak, in the little ways I know
Will learn to battle young and soon take heed.
I know when cherry buds learn to obey
The gusty April rain drops stern command;
I know that night will usher into day
Sun gems of dew drops to bestrange the land.
I know the lark will rise in afterglow
Of storm…proud wings above the scarlet lea;
And a river young will wear a way to go
Until it cuts a channel to the sea.
Batter me down, Life! Give me blow for blow!
I'll take the bleeding lips and liberty!

TO A DISSATISFIED

Fight on, clean spirit! Fight thy liberal way,
Though bursts no dawn behind these prison cells;
Fight on as though young flesh will soon decay
While wrestling with a thousand earthly hells.
And too, those friendly demons, saint of face,
Did mark you young and well and living strong,
Then smote your freedom with a servile trace
When caging you with a low world's lifeless throng.

Now every tremor in your youthful breast
Blood warm, reverberates in my own,
To see you living silent in unrest,
You of high blood who battles life alone.
I'd give my life for Life to set you free,
And risk Proud Death's uncertain liberty.

TO EDITH

Do you remember April evenings when we
Tripped side by side on tender orchard grasses
Beneath the spreading lime white apple tree?
Do you remember night birds' fluttering passes
Into shower drenched wind quivering leaves?
And the cloud patched sky, the wry face moon
And sleeping valley mists do you remember? It grieves
Me to forget…our lives broke then…broke soon,
Too soon we drifted down corridors of Time
With new lovers following after…and now
The grass is dead, the winter's rainy slime
Marks jet black each leafless apple bough.
Can you remember a dread that banished?
A love that faded?…a joy that vanished?

MY MOUNTAIN HOME

Deserted now you stand with lichened walls
Mouldering into dust. Your window panes
Are shattered by reckless winds and rains.
Your birds and bats will come when darkness falls.
Once we gathered in your eerie halls
To share life's meeker gifts of joys and pains,
But now my folks are gone. Still your remains
Abide with me when your haunting spirit calls.
Even your yard trees whisper from their height.
They see my eyes heavy lidded, wet with dreams;
They see my candle soul send forth its beams
And wonder if I shall share the coming night.
But oh this place is lonesome, lonesome here,
And no one, oh no one anymore goes near.

CLEAN FINGERS SLOPED IN FAREWELL

Sloped in farewell their clean straight fingers
When Elizabeth took his hand for long parting,
Knowing the swift hour John would be starting
Where the only earth is reef that lingers
In the warm black water of southern seas.
Elizabeth: could she forget when the evening stars
Shone clear above Ohio's white sand bars?
No, not John, nor his land with willow trees.

John: could he forget when the sandals of pain
Thwarted the very steps he was taking?
Willows, white sand, stars, fell like Autumn rain
On his shoulders. Yet memories kept waking
His brittle brain. The nights he lived again
With Elizabeth, the restless sea kept breaking.

TO A GEORGIAN LASS

A gusty wind spread like a silver sail
Through poplar leaves. The varying monotones
Of wind in trees, the listless blue, the frail,
Slow change of skies, the weaving pine tree cones;
They halt our merry youth in Nature's garden.
We knew for Time, there was no turning back.
How soon footprints on the earth would harden
To leave our silence in the frozen black.

We mingle Mae with the elements to find
New life when the rain drips from a cedar bough
You know, you love a silver sheet of wind
More than an ardent lover's mutual vow.
You know, you love high clouds, flying thinned,
More than a kiss upon your lips or brow.

WHERE I WAS BORN

This is the place where I was given birth:
Where these vine clad trees stand in a row.
It is the place, for mother told me so
Before I left home. This was our hearth,
This frescoed stone. Here words of mirth
Were spoken by the kindred ties I know.
And it was more than twenty years ago!
I can scarce believe this thin sward of earth
Cradled me when I was very young,
For now tall locust trees are matted here;
And only strangers any more go near,
And the toads, the bats, and rain drops among
The ruins. And I was born where one dim path
Furrows the thorny hands of aftermath.

MARGARET

Her eyes were dreamy pools under long lashes,
Brown as the magnolia's sun-kissed leaf;
Her countenance was beautifully brief
And swift as summer stars' meteoric flashes
Down to the silent rim of trees; and high
And blemishless was her proud character.
All the pride of beauty yielded to her
As the full moon to the starry sky.
She would saunter off when the full moon rays
Shone on Spring's snowy rows of apple trees
And listen to the night wind harmonies,
Knowing beauty is all that really pays.
When my soul is empty and hope withdrawn,
She beams a jewel on the breast of dawn.

RETURNED

If one swift-breathed yesterday I could recall
Time would be springtime in sunny Tennessee
When eerie birds sing in the boughs to solace me,
And clouds blow westward over Lincoln Memorial–
To see a sickle moon caught in a windy tree,
To walk old roads curved into tree-lined places,
To visit favorite haunts, to familiar faces,
Live now as I did then and feel at least as free.

Then fellow to fellow we would meet sure at last
Where in this materialistic void one spark
Of beauty vies the bleak sonorous endless dark
Where Time has blown not many youthful years but fast.
Then let this be the dream I build in which to die:
Live in beauty with friends and daff the mad world by

A SKEPTIC'S PLEA

If there is life beyond this life, let it
Be this: The friendly Earth my boyhood knew
With quaint old upland peach trees in the dew;
High wind, a gust of rain, a shattered bit
Of Heaven in a sleepy willow brook;
Old friends I know, a mother's daring smiles,
All the gentleness of those old afterwhiles
I'd love; but not the dance with Death I took.

Let me express but this, my vain regret:
That I be born of woman once again;
Know tawny flesh, this same rebellious brain
That guides me on the streets of life; and yet
I pine not for one day that I have lost.
The past is past, why stop to count the cost.

SILENT EARTH

How silent, the countless billions who have died.
They cannot speak to tell us where they lie.
We who tramp above them. how are we to know
Who lie beneath our feet where sawbriars grow?
We only know men born are men to die,
And they too will ride, if the dead must ride,
Out past all space and where all time is vain;
Where their rich dust will be a hidden urn
That will not hear, nor see, nor even know
If the beat upon their face is rain or snow.
Why should it matter? They cannot return
When they have given up the body and the brain.
Yet deceiving is this epitaph I found:
"How soft and sweet is sleep beneath the ground."

HEAVEN ENOUGH

Heaven for me will be an April field
With an orchard wind striding gallantly.
Heaven will be new Nature's rarest yield
Each tree will be a gusty rain beat tree
Heaven, I know, will have the wooded hills,
White cherry sprays, one long shrill note of sun,
The cloudless blue, the silver singing rills,
The laughing crow…but not oblivion…
Not mine the clean white robes that angels wear:
Not mine the stern oblivious paradise…
Fantastic world for saints with golden hair,
For ultra good, for parasites and the wise.
An April field is Heaven enough for me
Where I may live forever friendless, free.

TO MUDDY WATERS

Muddy waters, how I have loved your crying,
Night and day, forever, past my open door,
Down through reckless channel breaks along the shore
Where winter wind in the ankle sedge is sighing.
And the infant moon circles low above the hills…
I've gone down at midnight and sat beside you
In woven reeds when the winter winds whistled through
Your lonesome bank-side trees; when your pulsing will
Was surging your body down a lost dark way.
Like some deep singer in the voiceless you fling
Futility to wind and march and sing and sing,
Perhaps songs built from new youth molding clay
While I return to the door where my cradle flame
Burns low, where the world shall know not my name

IT WILL NOT MATTER MUCH

Does it matter in what lover's arms I've lain
On ominous nights when silence brooded on
Night's velvet dusk, when moon mist of river dew
Meshed the poplar leaves with soft tints of rain?
And does it matter what lover's lips mine touch
If they have grown old with love, if they are clean?
Who will know when marks of lips are left unseen
And lovers soon forget? It will not matter much.
Age, Youth's foe, will come in his bewildered flight
And greater sweethearts and friends like morning fog
Drawn by a lonesome moon from some prairie bog
And sent into the finalities of an August night.
Alas for those who never give their heart and mind;
Life is more fickle, perverse, far more unkind.

THE WIND HAS WAYS

The wind has ways in little woods I know,
Miraculous, subtle, stealthy, divine…
The wind the common voice where dumb plants grow,
The wind humanistic as bladeless vine…
He is a hound dog nosing by my door at night
Snapping his teeth in delicate tunes of deceit
He will dance with lovers in the pale moonlight,
Then crouch to space to rest his tired feet.
The wind has ways when he is a man of war
To paste cold clammy fingers in the eyes
Rebellious men saber him never to scar
When the wind's way is the way to despise,
The wind's last way when we lie down to sleep
May be our errand boy on the boundless deep.

LOUISE

Why should you let your fervent thoughts pursue
Earthly elements of wind and rain? Your rare time
Is wasted there. Winds blowing above us chime
Forever the same tune while life is brief as dew.
Earth is always young. His beauty will not fade.
The lilt of swinging leaves and summer moons return
And like Indian Summer leaves, our life days burn
With candle flames. One wind gust, our dreams are made.
Lovers and friends won't they remember ties
Of loyalty? Earth heeds not to these but lends her room
For your wind bitten cross. Your youthful bloom
Is crushed to dust, a wind-mark under murky skies
While time will be slow to resurrect you again;
Earth prides you with her elements of wind and rain.

OLD LOWLAND MEADOWS

I am not beauty mad when thus I sing:
Old lowland meadows have more charm for me
Than any colored landscape in the spring,
When cattle wade in grass above the knee,
And there are little leaves and lesser sun;
When kildees bravely singing skyward fly;
Where dreamy silver streamlets leap and run,
And batteries of clouds flaunt cross the sky.
Believe me there is charm when old lost pride
Of human, cattle, grass, turn life again,
Forgetting the blank, desolate country side
And the ominous patter of her winter rain.
Yes, there is charm when spring is in the boughs,
When kindred beast to kindred beast makes vows.

TWO LIVES

If I'm not dead before the morning sun comes up,
Some swift breath yesterday I left behind
Will come and cut and scar itself across my mind.
Then I drink from my cup of loneliness and sup
To bitter dregs. Why should this be and why–
When I've loved my youth, my life, and every joy
That counts; when I've lived life as any boy.
How can it be. I ask…Two lives is one reply.
I see my stalwart limbed superbly made
Eleven strike terror down the battered field;
I see a death punt blow some stubborn toe did wield.
They fight, they drive, flinch not, for they are unafraid.
And I belong to them, but moods in curious books
Allure me far, with pen, to lonesome moonlit nooks.

HARVARD OR THE SEA

I have lived my youth in one unsettled state
And months of barren earth is life too much for me.
The glorious close will bring me Harvard or the sea.
Nine months earth prisoned! How can I bear to wait?
Since I was twelve, I have been foot free to the soil;
Pocketless a dime, I've rambled through many a town
When the winter moon and silver stars slanted down;
Bunked with toughs; did with them a tremendous toil;
Met pals, forgot; stopped and took my school life stay.
Now within Harvard's Halls there is one life for me.
Another life is on waste water's blue immensity
That will make me turn my back on home, forget the day
My feet were bound to earth. Then Great Seducer Sea,
Be last to pant and lick your wet lips over me.

TO CALLOYE

Calloye, since sleepless nights I have forgotten you
As trees forget the winter wind's harsh searing cries,
Your smiles I have forgotten and your midnight sighs.
They mean no more to me than the cool rain dripping through
The cedar tops on some soft windless August night.
Why now remember your last laughs and the dripping rain
And the last long loneliness when in my arms you've lain
Until morning? How can I wage a single fight
Against our enemy, Old Memories? Why not a kiss
Of mine, a clasp of finger tips? For they will stay
With us, I think, perhaps, forever and a day;
When we have gone fickle and forgot decaying bliss.
Calloye, remember, life's more perverse for woman
Who holds to fire, beauty, and lives divine human.

PERSONAE

I.

The frosty moon swam high above this mountain home
Moulting to hoary mists, wide heaths, lean fields, and trees;
Night winds sang through stripped branches wild harmonies.
Stars wove fantastic patterns on high Heaven's dome;
Above his home's blue finger rims of pine tree lace.
This was his light of birth, the sword his youth had known
With books, bread, water, stars, snowdrifts in silence blown;
The crow's deep clarion call, the river's starry face…
All these became a part of changeful youth that grew
To man that nature called her own: free space, sheer sun,

Love for life's lowly forms that cannot speak aloud;
The shaggy beasts that plow the hillside world into
The need of man…undoing life that when undone
Is drab…gone swifter than the passing of a cloud.

II.

When summer drouths have struck pestilence-stricken hills
Where the father's rude plowshare has broken stubborn roots
Unlacing the universe in search of fruits sweeter
To garner least the wintry wind's high lonesome chills,
Blow loud incessant sounds unto the lattice door
Where last the hungry wolf bends down in subtle pride
To children shivering before the wood fireside,
Waiting the gifts done flown with drouth before.
Thus bounteous our gifts some beauty fades away
The gaunt wolf snapping at his children by the door,
To man instinctive as the vulture's circling veer
Down thorny piers of clouds so deathless molten gray…
The father feels a keen hurt in his bosom's core.
His brittle brain went snap…the gray perhaps is near.

*Plum Grove Church
and Plum Grove Cemetery.*

*Jesse Stuart at Robert
Burns' birthplace, autumn, 1937.
Jesse lived in Scotland one year.*

Harvest of Youth

Jesse and his mother,
Martha Hylton Stuart

Mitchell Stuart
(Jesse's father)

HARVEST OF YOUTH

Since I am young I'll sow my seeds
    In earth with passion burning white…
My bleeding hands the thorny weeds,
    My lips a mad man's curse to night.

My flesh may thin until it reels,
    The recompense for happy pain…
Wind hounds may chase and bite the heel
    Of this young braggart sowing grain.

But:
When Time reclaims his barren field
    He will not question nor disown,
If your fruit gave the sweetest yield,
    If my seed were the wildest sown.

FOREKNOWN

What is last year's rain to you
    And what is last year's snow
Same as any tender flame
    That flares before you go?

What are yesterdays to you?
    What are the songs you sing?
A smile, a tear, maybe a sigh,
    Perhaps not anything.

LIFE'S INCONSTANCY

I think that life's inconstancy
    Is much like April rain;
Descending from swift daring clouds
    Just to return again.

CREED

To any lover give your heart
And let each wanton kiss sear deep;
For love will tread above your head,
When lips are colorless in sleep.

TO A WOMAN IN BLACK

Gaze not on his vacuous whiteness
    Since he is dead.
To other youth why now confess
    The words he said?

Empty of love for you he dies
    Pained and deep.
Beneath the wintry earth he lies
    And you: why weep?

YOUTH

As pollen returns to fragrance
And rose petals return to dust;
Youth will push ever onward,
Only because they must.

SAINT OR SINNER

You tell me with two eyes like stone
That I am a rugged sinner;
That I shall know by bending bones
When you pass me by the winner.

Since we are fruit of a human tree
And death frost blights our common lot,
To cling or fall is same to me
When saints dry up, when sinners rot.

HURT NOT THE PROUD

Hurt not the proud for they shall live
    Enduring strangely quiet alone;
They who were proud words in flesh
    Shall surely carve proud words in stone.

WORDS

Words are like birds
Going to the south;
They will return again
With love in the heart
And song in the mouth.

MY FIRST TRUE LOVE

Where Sandy waters surge and flow
    Past a mossy cot and lea,
Is where we said the last farewell
    That parted Edith and me.

The night was fair, the mountain mist
    Was barrier for the moon;
Little thought we the parting hour
    Would break our lives too soon.

Oh madden lips and laughing eyes!
    I would they could never
Steal care and bliss of happy youth,
    Bliss, and bliss forever.

That night I left the mossy cot,
    The moon was sinking low
Above the hills God made his own
    Where Sandy waters flow.

I left the youth in life I love,
    The fairest of the fair;
My spirit would not bend to her:
    I could not tarry there.

Her eyes were blue as violet blue;
    Her spirit was the hills;
She was as free as May wind in
    A world of daffodils.

O cot of dreams! Oh God of love!
    Wherever love may be;
Discard the wrath and give me faith,
    Why not abide with me?

But now the years are winging by;
    My youth begins to change;
And many a lover I have had
    And yet I find them strange.

And when I think of my first Love,
    There come these scenes to mind;
The peaceful lea, the mossy cot
    And girl I left behind.

Where Sandy waters surge and flow
    Past mossy cot and lea;
Edith lives with her next true love
    And still remembers me.

SIN

Better are young men who have sinned:
    They set their feet on firmer sod;
For like young trees bend to the wind
    They too will know and yield to God.

PITY ME NOT

Pity me not
When the day is done;
All is forgot
With the morning sun.

After the night
Of the dark and rain,
Life will grow bright
With sunrise again.

ONE LIFE

One life
Is a wisp of fog
Between eternities…
No second choice, for Death wipes the
Slate clean.

IMMODESTY

Miss Poplar Tree is first to gem
    Fair April's sunlit land;
She wears a dress with leafy hem
    And waves her wedding hand.

And when Old Summer Sun gets high,
    She finds tranquil repose;
But let Young Silver Wind come by,
    She ruffles up her hose.

LINCOLN WEEPS

The rain is softly falling
Where Ann Rutledge lies;
A voice is sadly calling
At the gray-moon rise.

The winds are faintly whining
Where Ann Rutledge sleeps;
The pine trees are a-pining
Where a tall man weeps.

SLEEP SPELL

Falls the rain, the rain is falling
    With a ghost-like sound,
Slow and steady, down, down…
    Through the low trees to the ground.
Whines the wind, the wind is whining
    Down the valley steep,
Swift the climb, and steep, steep…
    Up dark mountains of sure sleep.

MY PEOPLE's PRAYERS

I always go to Plum Grove Church
To hear my people's prayers;
I know here is religious air
For the mood of God is theirs.

Even the side lamps' dingy flames
Are low red moons on the wall;
Without, the dreary dark expanse
Covers the trees, the field and all.

When I see my aged blood bow,
I hear my father's prayer
To his far gold-domed Heaven,
Expectant somewhere, somewhere…

But mother makes my blood drip cold
With bowed head aging white,
When she prays in solemn prayer:
"God, where is my boy tonight?"

WARNOCK BLUES

Not for a wee cot on a hill
    In the eerie month of June,
Not for a silver winding rill
    Nor a slice of mellow moon;

Not for the love of a mild maiden
    Painted by watery reeds;
Why this when my heart is laden
    With the Past until it bleeds.

And not for a day of life I spent
    Behind the shadowy blind;
Little to me the days have meant…
    I leave them far behind.

Then what is it I am after
    To curb my wanderlust?
To me pain is only laughter
    When droning through the dust.

CARVER LIFE

When I was young I went to Carver
To tramp the lilac square;
Where all the gloom was lilac bloom,
Where girls were passing fair.

I was a lad free as the wind;
For I had been a rover.
But I sat down in Harrow town
And soon became a lover.

I made my vows like a fool for love
I kept vows under cover;
If Love was late, I would not wait,
I found another Lover.

With Love for this, with Love for that,
With Love for everything;
Free as the wind, why should I mind
What future years would bring?

But the years went slow at Carver:
Alas there came the day,
When like a lad, I felt full sad
To pack and go away.

So I am here, my Loves are there
Carver is far away;
They must not doubt, that I'm not out
With other girls today.

For Fairfield has lovely gardens,
She has her lilac square,
Where hours I know, will sweeter grow
When I meet my True Love there.

Yet I make vows like a fool for Love,
I keep vows under cover;
If she is late, I will not wait,
I'll seek another Lover.

COOL FINGERS IN FAREWELL

Sad is our parting,
    Sad and as long–
Through decades so lonely–
    Sad as my song.
Like an awakening
    That came at dawn;
Voices the last parting…
    Silence prolong.

Never more together,
    Now words are vain;
Can the heart be mended
    Or body's pain?
She shall never linger
    On my last day–
Just to say a farewell,
    Then go away.

Reality image
    Forever past;
Leaving a lost lover–
    Hopes all are blast.
My darkness…her morning–
    Morning anew;
My cross and my Heaven–
    Only…Adieu!

Thus cometh two seasons,
    Dun hours…and bright;
Days briefly, prismatic
    Swift, Swift the night.
When shadows are falling
    Near my hearth fire,
Sad songs I'll be humming–
    The wind my lyre.

Seeking out loneliness,
    Divergent stars;
Then why we remember
    Secrets and bars?
Now this our last parting
    Sad hearts can tell–
I offer cool fingers
    In last–Farewell.

EMPTY LOVER

Go lass, so willingly possessed
    Of virgin beauty;
Go pant beneath a lover's breast,
    It is your duty.

Give flesh and limb your empty breath
    In stifled laughter;
Through life you'll walk alone; in death
    No one mourns after.

STANZA ON LEAVING COLLEGE

(Written In Dejection)

My room lights sink, outside the night winds moan;
The hour approaches I strike the world alone.
Then forget me not for I shall think of you,
And this my last dear friends, adieu! adieu!

DISILLUSION

Go sing your songs in your cities of tin,
    Go sing the hell of your creedful days;
Go strike a thunder to embitter Sin,
    Go live a life of parasitic praise.

Maybe the anarchist who bled your sod
    With Sin in the detriment of sorrow,
Will laugh in the face of your pageant God
    When he rides on the winds of tomorrow.

WEATHER

In eerie months we proudly went
    Down on the verdant banks of Clyde,
To sit beside the laughing stream
    Which was the youthful lover's pride.

When now we go to ruthless Clyde
    Her inky banks are lost in snow.
We miss the place where once we sat
    And what forgotten sweethearts know.

Then bonnie Clyde will surely tell
    Youth's differences in weather.
Not winter gray, but fragrant May,
    When we put our lips together.

NOVEMBER NIGHT

I shall remember this moon
    Low burning on a dusky world and up the evening sky.
I shall remember at noon,
    In the morning, and at other times when November winds pass by.

I shall remember this night;
    The recurrent loneliness, you, and the heavy words you said,
I shall regard with delight
    These bearable words and you, after I'm long, long dead.

TENNESSEE FARMER

Ott Davis spent his life on his farm:
    In Tennessee he died.
In Tennessee they buried him
    Where pasture winds defied;
His entire life was freely spent
    On his poor, pine-tree farm;
The weird bells of his upland sheep
    Ring not to do him harm.

His children, Mary, Rube, and Glennis
    Rotate wheat, rye and cane;
While tall pine trees grow with the weeds–
    Despite the wind and rain.
He sleeps in shadows of the pines–
    With epitaphs on his tomb;
His children follow in his steps–
    Are going to their doom.

ALOHA

Dark sheets of night are gathering fast
And lightning streaks the darkening vast
While fighting winds the wild woods quell
That mournfully speak a sad farewell.

And now up near the troubled sky
Three kildees meet and part, but why?
It is but this: I know they tell
In words their own a long farewell.

Still on beyond the downland sheep,
Low to the wind strange calls for sleep;
By the tinkling of each silver bell
That kindly says to me…farewell…

It may be long before I see
These starry skies of Tennessee;
Although this night when starlight fell
I linger'd long to say…farewell…

MY BROTHERS

I am wondering tonight, dear brothers,
If you hear the patter of windless rain
Beating cold Flanders sod and dying grass
Where slowly you gave up the body's pain.

I wonder if your deep sleep is ever
Broken by dreams of the remembered past;
Shrapnels flying, barbed wires, winter trenches;
Truck trains, red horizons, and artillery blast.

And the crush of cities forever doomed;
Desolation that followed the front line trench;
Shelled houses, barricades, trees splintering down
And ungathered lads between two fires, the stench.

And now America calls you, your home,
Loved ones, but you sleep. All words are vain.
Did you think back of clean beds, mother, sisters,
And wonder if all would ever happen again?

Now on your graves tall trees are growing,
Your names are untold on crosses weathered black;
How great the change, dear brothers, we thought
All, or surely one of you, would be coming back.

But in Flanders fields you sleep, my brothers,
Herbert, Milton, Lee, you went, I had to stay,
When Life is won by losing, lost by keeping,
And being young, I had to see him march away.

MY HOUSE

My house stands by an autumn fringe of wood,
    Weather-beaten, a forlorn, desolate shack–
Behind my house a heavy corn crop stood;
    Before a treeless hill is drabbish black.

One hundred yards away Muddy River runs
    Northward–turns eastward at a willow bend.
Here from my door I've seen one thousand suns
    Twist strangely down at the day's slow end.

And in this desolate valley not so wide
    As to set a house, to have a garden land.
I have found tranquility that will abide,
    I have found love for the stranger's hand.

So I am content with living here alone,
    My work the candle the written page;
My Loves: a flower complete, a voiceless stone,
    And yellow leaves from some forgotten sage.

FINISH

Bury me where the pine trees' scattered cones
    Lay withered on some desolate hill;
Leave me with earth's thin wrapper on my bones
    Where tame hands fear to pluck the first jonquil.

Here silent earth will grip my rebel breath,
    And there will be blind sickness here for men;
My wine blood will flow to the mouth of Death
    And he will taste but fear to drink it then.

Then shovel deep my brown rebellious flesh
    To lie forever cold where last it fell;
Dust from the lowly elemental mesh,
    Gone for the last long sleep and to fare well.

SCARS

With life's pitcher broken at the fountain
Spilling sweet wine of youth to Mother Earth,
Will we forget that sin…or remember
The demon walking by our side from birth?

Does it matter much who lives, we question…
In either world…if wars be waged? Our stars
Shall brand our courage, skill and usefulness;
The Prince-of-Peace will know us by our scars.

SPRING COMES

Spring comes in her green armor clad
Ushering light into her day;
Winter has made the blithe heart sad,
But Spring will make the sad heart gay.

SHE VENTURED FAR FROM GOD

She ventured far from God in unseen ways
Like a drooping willow stung by winter rain.
She lost clean friendship of her girlhood days
And thought the future would not welcome her again,
A girl once steeped in muted corridors of sin.

Like the willow tree when verdant April came,
Sick of the past she staggered back to spring.
New life put forth when she lost her winter name.
Old friends thought the willow tree a lovely thing
Flowering by the water in April blossoming.

FUGITIVE

He is a fugitive lying here alone
So lifeless now tawny flesh he bore;
Decaying strangely into earth and stone
Like his rude sires who have gone on before.

He sleeps a fugitive…and let him be…
He sleeps…he bothers not his own proud kin…
He lies beneath his black-jack saplin tree
Where knotty roots and moles are prying in.
The toad on dewy nights hops in the grass
Upon the black sod where they left him lie.
The silly sheep penetrate the jungle mass
And wings, the owl beneath the star-lit sky.

Now since he rests a dreamer–wake him not…
Let him dream on beneath his black-jack tree,
Dream of his dame, his hounds, warriors, his cot…
Realities with God in his eternity…

The tall rag weeds climb up his cabin door;
His hound dogs went in search for greater game;
His powder horn rusts on the puncheon floor…
The Red Man's gone…the timber wolf is tame…

He will not wake though woodland saps return
And leaves adorn each gentle swaying limb;
Tho dead, the passions in his breast must burn
For days when life was surely sweet to him.

Let him sleep on…don't break his warring dreams…
And God, let him still keep his pride 'round him;
He loves the shrill defiant panther screams
In a world where his deers and elks have found him.

Jesse on his way to mail the
manuscript of "Man with a Bull-Tongue Plow."

Honest Confession
of a Literary Sin

Jesse Stuart

Jesse, as a young educator

Foreword

Harvest of Youth, my first book of poems, was privately published by Scroll Press, Howe, Oklahoma in 1930, I didn't welcome this book the moment I laid eyes on a copy. Although I had agreed to pay $150 for 300 copies, I paid $100 down and received my first 50 copies. When I received these 50 copies, as disappointed as I was, I knew I would not be paying them $50 more and getting 250 more copies of the book. I knew that I had been swindled.

Our local county newspaper, *Greenup County News*, gave it a review, local boy makes good, gets his first book published. V. L. Sturgill, an English teacher in the Ashland City Schools, Ashland, Kentucky, gave it a good review. "V. L.," eleven years my senior, whom I held as an idol after hearing him read poetry at a Greenup City High School assembly. *Harvest of Youth* got a review or two—maybe three or four—in small poetry magazines where I had submitted some of my early poems, written in high school, steel mills, army barracks, and in college.

I had selected from over 500 early poems and put this book together in 1929 when I was 22. It wasn't published until 1930 after I had borrowed $100 from Uncle Andy Johnson, a farmer, to make my first payment. I wasn't known at our local bank. I didn't have any securities and I didn't have anybody to go my Security if I tried to borrow money at our local bank. But I was like so many young and older people then and now. I wanted my first book published.

I liked to write and I had done much writing for my age but I didn't know how to prepare a manuscript and submit it to a publisher. Still, I'd had a great creative writing instructor at Lincoln Memorial University, Harry Harrison Kroll, who was getting his novels published. He knew how to prepare a manuscript and send it to a publisher, but never taught us this important part of creativity, as I teach participants in my classes today. Had I but known how to do this, my early publishing might have been a different story. My *Harvest of Youth*, according to critics many years later, might, with a little editing by a good editor, have been accepted on a royalty basis. Whether this could have been true or not, is supposition. One can only surmise, fathom a guess, speculate by reading what is in it now.

I was really ashamed of my first book. It was published without a dust cover. There wasn't a single comment by a critic published in the book about what anyone had said about the merits of my first poems. I knew by reading well-published books, by name publishing houses of that day and time, that my first published book was all wrong and I didn't want this. I wanted a good name house, who published the well-known writers of the day–and to be published on a royalty basis like Carl Sandburg, Robert Frost, and Sherwood Anderson.

So I gave away a few copies of this book to my friends, three of them to former teachers. One man didn't keep his, but an elementary teacher and high school teacher kept theirs. One returned her book thirty years later to our daughter. I gave one to a business manager of Lincoln Memorial, who was a friend, and had been kind to me when winter weather was so terrible I couldn't work outside and almost defaulted on my payments to Lincoln Memorial University. I worked all my expenses there and being a strong young man I did hard work–certainly not hours in a warm library where I'd liked to have worked with books. The book I gave to the business manager of Lincoln Memorial University ended up after his death in a trash can on the Lincoln Memorial University campus.

Roger Smith, a classmate, found it in the trash can. He said: "Stuart may not be much of a writer but I can't stand to see his book treated like this. I've worked many a day with him on the LMU campus." And, he certainly had. He later sold this book. It's one of the two found books that have been sold for $1,000.00. V. L. Sturgill, a year before this sale, sold his copy for $900.

The year after *Harvest of Youth's* publication, 1931, I entered Vanderbilt University where it seemed to me everyone in the Fugitive Group, plus faculty members and others were writing books and getting them published. These were hard-cover books with dust covers, published by well-known houses on a royalty basis. Among these writers were: John Crowe Ransom, Merrill Moore, Robert Penn Warren, Donald Davidson, John Donald Wade, Edwin Parks, Allen Tate, Laura Riding, Caroline Gordon (who was at this time Mrs. Allen Tate), Dr. Edwin Mims (Chairman of the English Department), and others.

Once, walking across the Vanderbilt campus with one of the best students in the English Department, one with whom I had four classes, we were discussing Vanderbilt writers and I said to him: "I'm a writer, too! I've written a book."

He stopped suddenly on the walk by old Wesley Hall (it burned a few days later) and looked at me. Of course, I stopped with him.

"What's the title?"

"*Harvest of Youth*. It's poetry."

"Who published it?"

"Scroll Press."

"I never heard of Scroll Press."

"It's at Howe, Oklahoma."

"Isn't that a vanity house?"

I didn't answer. We walked on in silence. But, we were friends later. I know He went to the library later and tried to find my book. After this experience, which embarrassed me and really cooled me, I knew I'd never tell another person I'd written a book until I had written one published by a good house on a royalty basis. Then, I'd shout it to the world: "I've written a book!" I also knew and I knew only too well, I'd kill *Harvest of Youth*. I'd murder my own book.

Shortly after I talked to my classmate on the street, I wrote a term paper, *Beyond Dark Hills*, for Dr. Edwin Mims. It was 322 typewritten pages from margin to margin. I did it in eleven days. I didn't know then it would be published six years later, 1938, as my third book under the same title. This book is still in stores today and first editions are collector's items.

Vanderbilt was the hardest year of my life. First semester I lived on 11 meals a week. Wesley Hall and the cafeteria where I worked burned and second semester I lived on a meal a day. I worked with a Methodist ministerial student as the only two student janitors at Vanderbilt. We worked four hours (we could finish in this time if we were lucky and worked hard and fast) each afternoon. Clem Carson, a classmate, loaned me his books. He and I had the same four classes. I couldn't buy textbooks.

At the end of the year I started writing poems at Vanderbilt. I borrowed two dollars and hitchhiked home at the end of the long year. I went home and farmed on my father's farm in the driest season in our history here. Our crops burned but I didn't care. From the time I came home I wrote poems as never before. They fell from my mind like autumn leaves from the trees, with little sticks on poplar leaves, I wrote, when I didn't have paper. And I was elected Superintendent of Greenup County Schools, 24 years old, youngest county superintendent in Kentucky's history. A depression was on. Our bank was closed. And we worked without pay. I wrote poems until January and I quit. I wrote a sheaf of 703 poems, which I called *Man with a Bull-Tongue Plow*–tied a hand towel around them, put them in the dresser drawer upstairs. I was unmarried and lived with my father and mother.

At the end of my year as Greenup County School Superintendent where I had made nearly as many vicious enemies as reforms (32 lawsuits) I resigned and went back to Nashville, Tennessee where I stayed at the YMCA. My expenses (lodging and food) were $2.00 per day. I wrote *Cradle of the Copperheads* which when revised 40 years later, typed 945 pages. In 16 months beginning with my term paper for Dr. Mims, I had written *Beyond Dark Hills*, which published at 399 pages, and *Man with a Bull-Tongue Plow*, 361 pages.

Cradle of the Copperheads has not yet been published.

After returning from Vanderbilt and putting all the remaining copies I had of *Harvest of Youth* in a fire under a large wash kettle where my mother washed clothes in our backyard, I did an article, which I called "Embryo," which meant to me infancy, and the beginning. This had to do with my literary sin, paying to have *Harvest of Youth* published. I'd taken only 50 copies of this book, one-sixth of the number I was to get. I'd payed $100 for these, a portion of the price I was to pay for the 300 copies I was to receive. But I had made a grave mistake of ever letting a few of these get out to friends who might hang onto them. I certainly didn't keep one myself. I had killed this book. I had destroyed it.

I sent "Embryo" out three times in 1933. It was returned from the magazines where I sent it. Then I laid it back in the bunkhouse, which my brother and I had built in our backyard, a building which still stands today. My father required all of us to go to bed at eight and get up at four. In the bunkhouse where we made coffee and sat up as long as we pleased, I wrote stories, poems, read books, and our mother used to often sit up with us, smoke with us, drink coffee and make quilts, dresses, shirts, and suits of clothes. Our mother was creative and could make about anything from cloth with scissors and thread and a sewing machine. Mom had her sewing machine in our two-room bunkhouse. She worked in my room.

I kept my books, typewriter, manuscripts, and letters in my room of the bunkhouse. I also brought my bride, Naomi Deane Norris, to this bunkhouse. She and I went over proofs of my first novel, *Trees of Heaven*, together in this bunkhouse. I had well-known guests in this bunkhouse, who walked the high hill path over and down from Greenup, Kentucky to see me. I also kept my rejected manuscripts here too, and among them was "Embryo." After three rejections I would send no more.

When E.P. Dutton published *Man with a Bull-Tongue Plow* it was widely reviewed as a "blockbuster" in poetry. It was certainly on the royalty basis. A first edition is now worth $300 if it has a dust cover and is in fair condition. (It was pirated and published in Japan in 1943 when they were at war with this country, 490 pages in translation. Dr. Hensley Woodbridge discovered this in 1975.) I didn't mind telling anybody I'd written *Man with a Bull-Tongue Plow*. I'd written it in 1932, the year I'd left Vanderbilt, in eleven months while farming and part of the time when I was county superintendent of schools. I'd destroyed all copies of *Harvest of Youth* I could get my hands on. I was sorry about the few copies I'd given away to friends. I was an author now and my first book was *Man with a Bull-Tongue Plow*. More book publications followed.

On October 14, 1939, Naomi Deane Norris and I were married. We renovated an old farmhouse, two-tenths of a mile away from my father's and mother's home and moved into it in autumn 1940. I had lived in this house from 9 to 12 years of age when my parents had rented it. Now I owned it. And we had more cattle, cows, and sheep than we had barn space for; so we kept four cows in this house while in other rooms we stored corn and hay.

When we moved here in 1940, 1 moved all my belongings from the bunkhouse: manuscripts, books, typewriter into one room of a four room square building I'd had built in our backyard. One of the other three rooms was used for a smokehouse, another for a tool shed, another for a wood shed.

As the years passed while we lived here, my books, magazines, and manuscripts expanded and took over the wood shed and tool shed, only the smokehouse was left of the four rooms. This is the way it is today, except in 1971 we built a large room over the garage and utility room and moved all the unpublished manuscripts upstairs to this big room well-heated and with modern facilities, where I do most of my writing today.

But there was a student getting his M.A. degree at Ohio University. He spent three years doing a thorough thesis on me. He was the one who resurrected *Harvest of Youth*. I hadn't killed it even though

I didn't have a copy of the book. I told him what I thought, but he told me facts were facts. He made it clear, in his thesis, that *Harvest of Youth* was my first book. Thus, it has been my first book since his thesis. (Lee Oly Ramey's "*An Inquiry into the Life of Jesse Stuart as Related to His Literary Development and a Critical Study of His Works*," Ohio University 1941, 271 pages.) I tried to get him to backtrack to convince him *Harvest of Youth* wasn't a book, but being an astute scholar he would have none of this. Facts were facts.

In 1956-57, I went back to McKell High School as principal after having served there four years in 1933-37. There were problems in this school and they couldn't get teachers. We used high school students to teach. All were carefully selected and did commendable work– one, Lee Pennington, was outstanding. One whole year he didn't attend a class but he taught. He is Lee Bowdin in my teaching novel, *Mr. Gallion's School.*

Lee Pennington was an excellent student. He was a top athlete in football, and he was a student spark which caused a troubled school to move in a positive direction. He liked his principal and I was fond of my student who was interested in writing. He was very good at folk music and in folklore. He was like a young, ambitious Greek of the Golden Age of Greece. While a student at McKell High School, he read many of my books which included *Man with a Bull-Tongue Plow* and *Album of Destiny*. He didn't know I had written *Harvest of Youth* and he never found it until he did his undergraduate work at Berea College. He was collecting books then and through Dr. Hensley Woodbridge, now my bibliographer, he obtained a photocopy of *Harvest of Youth* done by University Microfilms. I never knew it existed.

Lee Pennington was 21 years old then. Reading *Harvest of Youth* "set him on fire." I was about 21 when I wrote many of the poems in *Harvest of Youth*. The poems in this book had more reader appeal for him than *Man with a Bull-Tongue Plow*, which I wrote when I was 24 and 25, more mature years. When Lee read this book, he wrote me an inspired letter saying youth should read it; and he had found out that the Council of Southern Mountains, then based at Berea College in Berea, Kentucky, was reprinting old books by people born in Appalachia–good books that should be printed again. Lee worked with Pearly Ayers, executive director of the council, and her secretary Ann Pollard. They agreed, after reading the book, it should be reprinted. At this time there were only three known copies of *Harvest of Youth*. Another one of the books to be reprinted was Harriette Simpson Arnow's *Mountain Path*.

I agreed to let them reprint *Harvest of Youth*, 2000 copies which were to sell for $3.00 per copy. It was simply reprinted from the old copy without dust wrapper. At first it was slow to sell until a modest dust wrapper adorned the old water-stained backs of the copy they photostated. After the dust wrapper, it sold out in two weeks. Now, a Council of Southern Mountains edition, if one can be found, sells for $50.00. Three small publishers since have wanted to reprint it. What makes a book go? Who will ever know? *Harvest of Youth* is youthful high school and college poems. Many don't know how I could have written them.

Lee Pennington and his wife Joy Stout, whom he married at Berea College when they were seniors there, went on to Iowa State University for graduate work. Both did their dissertations on my work. Joy did her thesis on my poetry. Lee did his thesis on the symbols in my poems in *Harvest of Youth*, which he set out to prove are in my novels. Lee's thesis was converted into a book, *The Dark Hills of Jesse Stuart*, which sold through three editions.

After all of this happened in regard to *Harvest of Youth*, I thought I'd better look up "Embryo," which was somewhere in the building in our backyard. This was in 1966. We didn't move the manuscripts inside until 1971. On the top of a stack of manuscripts, I found it. The top sheet was barely discernible. The front door of this room had a space over it even when closed, a space that allowed wrens to come in and build nests. I never objected. I worked at my desk in summer when wrens flew in barely over my head to feed their young, in nests on my manuscripts and books. There was a hole under the door (both holes later corrected) that allowed Old Ben, a black-snake, to come in (he later became a pet). Wrens didn't like him, but I made him behave.

On the top of the manscript "Embryo" was so much wrens' droppings where they had alighted, the page was almost indiscernible. It had to be dried out in the sun before I could scrape it off. Then I revised it and gave the manuscript a new title, "Honest Confession of a Literary Sin." I had the manuscript retyped. My typist was amused with the stains on the first page. I sent it once to the *Saturday Review of Literature*, a magazine I had once written for, but now all had changed because it was mostly staff written. "Honest Confession of a Literary Sin" didn't fit into the new editorial policies of the *Saturday Review of Literature*. I sent this manuscript there October 11, 1966. In October 1976, exactly ten years later, I sent the article again to my friend Al Abrams. It was accepted, an article 43 years old. Proof of what I have always told my creative writing participants in colleges and universities in the United States and a few foreign countries. Always hang onto your old manuscripts.

Greenup, Kentucky
December 1, 1976
Jesse Stuart

Jesse Stuart and his bride, Naomi Dean Norris (Jean Torris in his poetry), pictured here at their home in W-Hollow in 1941.

Honest Confession of a Literary Sin

by Jesse Stuart

In 1928 when I was a senior at Lincoln Memorial University, Harrogate, Tennessee, I became very ambitious and wanted to publish a book of poems. I was, at that time, twenty-one years of age; it seemed that I was getting old enough to do something. I had written hundreds of poems. I had seen myself in print in only a few small poetry journals, journals that expected to make the contributors pay for publishing the magazine. The acceptance propositions were put to the contributors like this: "We expect you to take so many copies of the magazine that your contribution is in, to defray expenses; or we expect you to subscribe to the magazine for one year." One realizes that the journals were not self-supporting; and if the contributors did not provide a little cash as well as poetry, the editors of these small magazines would have had to pay for everybody's publishing besides their own.

I grew tired of paying to see myself in print. My young vanity evaporated. The heat passed off as the money went out of my pocket. I began to cool. I thought that if I were to pay to see myself in print, I would pay to have a book published. I Would have a book of my own to hold in my hands and to admire. It would do me good to see a book of my own upon a shelf. I was old enough to do something– twenty-one years old, with only contributions to small magazines. I began to look around for a publisher.

A publishing house in the South offered to publish my book for two-hundred dollars. I was to get twelve free books and three announcements in a small poetry journal. The rest of the books were to be kept by the company and sold at two dollars each. I was to get one-third of that amount if they sold. I talked to my former teacher and writer friend of mine. He laughed and said, "It looks pretty steep to me. If you pay for your vanity, you should have it along to show, and not to let the other fellow show it."

I immediately dropped all correspondence with this publisher and went West. In the West I found a publisher with a different proposition. He offered to publish a one-hundred page book and make three hundred copies of the book for one-hundred and fifty dollars. It looked like a fine proposition to me. I told him to send me sample copies of the paper covering the backs–send me a sample of his work–send me a contract, for I was in a hurry. He complied with my requests, and I sent one-hundred dollars to him with the contract signed.

The summer had passed–another autumn–and another summer had come before I had found my publisher. The contract was signed in the summer of 1929. I negotiated with my publisher all winter and it was in August, 1930, before I received a copy of my first book. I shall never forget the day I received that first copy.

I was in entirely different surroundings and among different people when I received it from the one I was in when I wrote the poetry and when the idea came into my mind to have a book published.

I had migrated over to Nashville, Tennessee, to Vanderbilt University with her "Fugitives" and with a name bigger than any school I had attended. It was the place I should go, I thought. And I made up my mind to teach school a year and then go back to Vanderbilt.

I had been at Lincoln Memorial when the idea came into my mind to have my first book published. I was on the Vanderbilt campus (not matriculated there–but only rooming there among Vanderbilt undergraduate and graduate students and going to school over at Peabody Teachers College) when I took the first copy of *Harvest of Youth* out of the mail. It was not the paper I had ordered at all. There was a different kind of paper on the back. The print was absolutely impossible. Loose threads ran through the back of the book. I handled it very carefully for fear it would fall to pieces. "If you pay for cheap things, you get cheap things," I thought.

I held the book in my arms as a mother holds her firstborn baby. I ran around showing it to three or four grey-headed professors not interested in poetry at all, and as they didn't want to embarrass me, they didn't comment. So I ran to a few women to show it, and they were no more sympathetic.

In the meantime, my publisher kept dunning me for the other fifty dollars, after he had released the first fifty books to me. He said that after I sent him the fifty dollars, he would send me the other two hundred and fifty books. I didn't send it because I didn't have the fifty dollars. I owed some bills I must pay out of my first teaching checks before I could pay him the other fifty. The hundred dollars I had sent him would have to be returned, for I borrowed that hundred from Andrew Johnson to have the book published. I thought I would sell enough of my books to pay the fifty dollars. I went to the local drug store in my hometown and told the owner I wanted to leave a few of them there for sale. I was teaching school then. I sold four out of the fifty–the druggist did rather. The books absolutely would not sell, regardless of the fine write-ups I got in two local papers.

I never was so ashamed of anything in my life as I was of that book. I didn't want one in my sight. In the meantime I had sent a few autographed copies out to little poetry journal editors telling them that I had appreciated their help by publishing some of my poetry in their journals. But now I was sorry for those things I had said. I was sorry a thousand times more, that I had ever paid to have a book published. I got one little review in a little Kentucky magazine. It was given to me because I was from the hill country of Kentucky and because the magazine was published in Kentucky.

My publisher kept writing me for the last fifty dollars, and I didn't know whether to pay him the last fifty dollars and not take the books for I had signed a contract with him to this effect. I wrote to my school teacher friend about it and He wrote back: "Hell no! Beat him. You have paid dearly for fifty books! That is enough of that vanity publicity! The fifty books are out against you now!" And he was right. If I could have, I would have taken a basket and collected all the books that were out against me and piled them in a heap before that publisher's eyes and said: "To hell with this low down vanity publishing. It sounds good–but to hell with it. I want you to see I don't want it. I want you just to see how you take your money from young would-be poets. Aren't you ashamed, swindling them the way you do? You should be if you are not. Putting this rotten trash out in book form–young, rotten work written on rotten paper–a heap of trash." And I would have loved to kick the ashes from these books into the wind and let the wind blow them into the publisher's face!

I do not blame him for publishing my book. He took my money and gave me nothing. It was my own fault. I was not old enough to see, or I had too much vanity in me to see, that if poetry isn't worth giving away it isn't worth reading. It should not be forced on the public. If it can't be sold it is all right to give it away–many good poems have been given away; of course, I don't propose to do that hereafter–because that is too cheapening for the artist–and then the postage comes out of his own pockets. But I realized I was not the only youngster who had done such a trick, for others had done the same thing; and many of them, I'll venture to say, were sorry. There was nothing I could do but make an open confession to this literary sin and say that, when I have to pay to have another thing published, I'll never be in print again. I mean positively what I say. Let others pay for having their poetry published if that is their only way. But if you ever see a book of verse of mine on the market, you can say it is one book of poetry the poet did not pay to have published.

I was angry with myself for having paid to have my own *Harvest of Youth* published, but as there wasn't anything I could do myself, I took my spite out on the publisher. I don't know what kind of letter I wrote him when I told him that I didn't want the other two hundred and fifty copies. I know I made the letter strong. I know I did write an article, "Stung by a Vanity Publisher," and sent it to *The Writer*. The editor wrote me a letter saying the article was too long to publish, but that he would like to take excerpts from it and publish them on the letter page. I wrote back and told him to go ahead and publish a part, if they couldn't publish all. I do not know if the article was ever published. I hope it was.

I know my first book was a hopelessly dead one. Only forty-five copies of it are left. The sooner they are destroyed, the better. I wish they were so many dead sticks in the woods. The water and the wind would soon destroy them then–and they would go back to earth as dirt, and I would not have anything to worry about.

If I have any advice to give a writer–young or old, but inexperienced, I would tell him not to let his vanity get away with him or the Vanity Publisher to get away with his pocketbook. The money is just as good to the would-be-writer as it is to the Vanity Publisher. I know of no better form of book racketeering than this. It is very well for those who have money to see their poetry in print, and for those who wish to pass their work on as a heritage to the family–but it is hell for a county youth to borrow money to have a book published and then have to pay the money back by teaching school and working as blacksmith in the steel mills. My intention is to be honest with you would-be poets and to tell you from my own inexperience; and from this experience, I say–avoid all vanity publishers. Don't pay any magazine to take your work.

Many poetry journals that do not pay for poetry, publish good poetry. They have excellent editorship! I certainly do not condemn them. But I do condemn magazines that feed on the vanity of youth and the vanity of inexperienced talent!

Vanity publishers cannot promote you at all. When they publish your work, all they have done is merely to publish it and get your money. You have to promote it. You have to sell it. If you are going to be an artist and if there is any real talent in you–certainly you will not think of such. I have hundreds of poems and sonnets in my possession now that I have written and kept–and hundreds have been destroyed–and I say to you that never will one of these be published if I have to pay for publication. I'll never give a book to the public again if I have to pay one cent to have it published. This is my honest confession to you.

Books of Poetry by Jesse Stuart

1. *Harvest of Youth*. 1930, the Scroll Press, Howe, OK. *Ibid.* 1964, The Council of the Southern Mountains Berea, Kentucky *Ibid.* 1998, The Jesse Stuart Foundation, Ashland, Kentucky

*2. *Man With a Bull-Tongue Plow*. 1934, E.P. Dutton, New York, New York. *Ibid.* 1959, E.P. Dutton.

*3. *Album of Destiny*. 1944, E.P. Dutton.

4. *Kentucky Is My Land*. 1952, E.P. Dutton. *Ibid.* 1987, The Jesse Stuart Foundation.

*5. *Hold April: New Poems*. 1962, McGraw Hill, New York, New York.

*6. *Autumn Lovesong*. 1971, Hallmark Publishing Company, Kansas City, Missouri.

*7. *The World Of Jesse Stuart: Selected Poems*. 1975, McGraw Hill.

*8. *The Only Place We Live*. By August Derleth, Jesse Stuart, and Robert E. Gard. 1976, Wisconsin House, Sauk City, Wisconsin.

*9. *The Seasons Of Jesse Stuart: An Autobiography in Poetry*, 1907-1976. 1976, Archer Editions Press, Lynville, Tennessee.

10. *Songs of a Mountain Plowman*. 1986, The Jesse Stuart Foundation.

*Out-of-print. All ten of these books, with the exception of *The Only Place We Live*, are available from the Jesse Stuart Foundation.